Mind Like Water

Other books by the author

What's the Rush?
Whale Done!

Mind
Like Water

*Keeping Your Balance
in a Chaotic World*

Jim Ballard

John Wiley & Sons, Inc.

To Sol

Illustration on page 84 copyright © 2002 by Jackie Aher.

Published by John Wiley & Sons, Inc., Hoboken, New Jersey
Published simultaneously in Canada

The author gratefully acknowledges the following for permission to quote from the following: "The Paradoxical Commandments" by Kent M. Keith are reprinted by permission. © Kent M. Keith 1968, 2001; Paramahansa Yogananda, *A World in Transition* (Los Angeles: Self-Realization Fellowship, 1999); Paramahansa Yogananda, *Journey to Self-Realization* (Los Angeles: Self-Realization Fellowship, 1997); Paramahansa Yogananda, *Songs of the Soul* (Los Angeles: Self-Realization Fellowship, 1983); Paramahansa Yogananda, *Undreamed of Possibilities* (Los Angeles: Self-Realization Fellowship, 1997); Paramahansa Yogananda, *Metaphysical Meditation* (Los Angeles: Self-Realization Fellowship, 1964); and Paramahansa Yogananda, *God Talks with Arjuna: The Bhagavad Gita* (Los Angeles: Self-Realization Fellowship, 1999).

For general information about our other products and services, please contact our Customer Care Department within the United States at (800) 762-2974, outside the United States at (317) 572-3993 or fax (317) 572-4002.

Wiley also publishes its books in a variety of electronic formats. Some content that appears in print may not be available in electronic books.

ISBN 0-471-08697-5

Printed in the United States of America

10 9 8 7 6 5 4 3 2 1

CONTENTS

FOREWORD

Over the decades that I've been privileged to work with thousands of individuals and organizations, I've continually been struck by the tendency of people to create problems by getting squarely in their own way. Since the human ego is the root cause of the problems we face on this planet, I figure the greatest single contribution any one of us can make toward solving the world's problems is to work within ourselves to rise above our own littleness and transform the way we see things. This is the whole point of Jim Ballard's wonderful book *Mind Like Water: Keeping Your Balance in a Chaotic World.* It's a set of tools that enables us to work within ourselves to clean up our own acts, so that we can be free to do the work we came to do in the world.

Ever since Jim and my friendship began almost thirty years ago, our shared concern with helping people relate better to themselves and others has led us to collaborate on a number of writing projects. Whether it was a business book *(Managing by Values, Everyone's a Coach,* or *Mission Possible)* or an attempt to influence the way people influence others at work and at home *(Whale Done! The Power of Positive Relationships),* it has always been a spiritually uplifting experience for us to work together. We begin all our writing sessions with prayer, asking the Great Writer to help us get our egos out of the way.

Jim Ballard's passion for helping people maintain calmness and balance in their life and work resulted in his writing *What's the Rush? Step Out of the Race ... Free Your Mind ... Change Your Life.* That book in turn led to his publishing an online biweekly newsletter, *The Balance Beam.* Virtually every person at the Ken Blanchard Companies receives and uses this resource; many of them give Jim feedback on how one or another issue of *Beam* has helped them toward equilibrium and perspective in their tasks. It was out of Jim's experience of writing *The Balance Beam,* and from his own inner work as a runner and a meditator, that this present book grew. I hope that you and countless other readers will find in *Mind Like Water* some ways to calm your mind and uplift your consciousness, and to transform the way you operate every day in this chaotic world.

Ken Blanchard

ACKNOWLEDGMENTS

My heartfelt thanks go to my best friend "home editor," and source of ideas, Barbara Perman. I am grateful to the many friends and subscribers to *The Balance Beam* newsletter, whose encouragement and support were so important to this book-writing endeavor. And to Margret McBride, my incredible agent, and to Tom Miller, my talented editor at Wiley, much warm appreciation.

For their guidance and inspiration, I wish to acknowledge the great line of masters: Jesus Christ, Bhagavan Krishna, Mahavatar Babaji, Lahiri Mahasaya, Swami Sri Yukteswar, and Paramahansa Yogananda. Jai gurus!

In the procession of the soul from within outward,
it enlarges its circles ever,
like the pebble thrown into a pond.

—EMERSON

INTRODUCTION

Because everything we do and everything we are is in jeopardy, and because the peril is immediate and unremitting, every person is the right person to act and every moment is the right moment to begin.

—Jonathan Schell

This is a book about change-making.

Everyone is coping with ever-increasing amounts of change these days. When change again and again threatens to throw our plans off kilter, we can become frustrated, stressed out, squeezed for time, pressed to do more with less. At such times it is tempting to see ourselves as victims of a runaway world. The tendency is to think that all change is something that happens *to* us, something we cannot predict or control.

That's why I'm excited about change-*making*—changes we ourselves initiate. We may have little or no control over the changes happening around us, but our real problem with handling turbulence is not what it seems to be. More accurately, it is not *where* it seems to be. It's not out there in the world of events and circumstances, but "in here," inside our heads, where we are constantly responding to the information our senses bring to us. The change-making this book talks about has to do with changing ourselves. Specifically, it's about achieving and maintaining balance in our lives and our work.

Balancing Act

When I was a kid the members of my gang of neighborhood boys often tried to impress each other with feats of skill and daring. A favorite was the balancing act. Walking a thin, horizontal edge of something provided an opportunity to demonstrate your courage and coordination—and also to become the object of taunting and teasing if you fell off. Walls, fences, railroad tracks, tree branches, log bridges over streams—anything that looked a bit dangerous and difficult was fair game. The thinner the beam and the greater the height, the better.

Nowadays as adults we're faced with a more daunting task—that of keeping our mental and emotional balance as everyday life whizzes on with unstoppable abandon. Given the demands of a busy, on-the-go lifestyle, each of us is required to be a tightrope artist again. Of the pitfalls with which our modern technological world is strewn, the loss of inner balance is perhaps foremost. To operate successfully amid a daily onslaught of change, each of us must work within the self to maintain calmness and centeredness.

This book will take you on a journey, a return to a lost country, an island of sanity in a storm-tossed sea of breathless, chaotic activity. Perhaps you are one of those who think that calmness and focus cannot be achieved in a world that has speeded up so disastrously in the past two decades. If so, your journey must begin with an honest appraisal of your attitude toward change.

The Runaround

When people describe the experience of being conned or taken advantage of, they often speak of being "given the runaround." It's a fitting term for the nature of these times. In addition to describing the perpetual hundred-yard-dash approach to life people are taking each day, it suggests that the element of deception is part and parcel of their response. The Runaround mentality might be expressed this way:

I have more to do and less time to do it. Nevertheless, I must still try to get everything done. The more change accelerates, the faster I must run. Thus I have no time to stop and consider whether there might be an alternative to the way I am living.

This painful soliloquy reminds one of the harried White Rabbit in Alice's adventures, whose response to her questions was, "No time to say Hello. Good-bye! I'm late, I'm late, I'm late!"

Perhaps the most alarming aspect of the Runaround trend is that it is being accepted as the inevitable lifestyle of the twenty-first century. This is not to say that many people are not bothered by the frantic pace of things. Vaguely uneasy about the speedup of their lives, they talk longingly of less fretful times. Nevertheless, like victims they accept a White Rabbit lifestyle as a condition of life. In so doing they contribute to a steadily growing pathology, a psychic landscape in which inner peace and calmness seem like bygone dreams.

Work and Home Runaround

Nowhere are the costs of the Runaround more painfully evident than in the workplace. Driven by demands for better quality, lower prices, and faster innovation, places of work generate unprecedented levels of stress. Workers and their employers pay for their loss of mental focus and emotional equilibrium in a variety of ways, including inattention, poor work quality, errors, stress, bad relationships, inaccurate decisions, lack of creativity, low morale, and the inability to self-manage or solve problems creatively.

Inevitably the pressures people experience at work ripple out to their families. Parents have less time to spend with their children. Their stress from work takes its toll on youngsters, who can be made to feel they are in the way when Mom or Dad comes home and needs time to relax. Weekends and vacations, far from offering opportunities to relax and get away from it all, become frantic catch-up times.

To be effective, working parents, as well as their bosses, associates, and employees, need specific tools and strategies for managing their inward mental-emotional climate. Equilibrium is vital to our success and enjoyment in work and life. As soon as inner poise is restored we're efficient, concentrated, creative, fun to be around. With its loss goes patience, focus, joy; everything seems more difficult and time-consuming.

About This Book

Mind Like Water assumes that while we may not have control over the events and setbacks that occur in our environment, there are simple methods all of us can use to impact our state of mind and personally avoid the Runaround. Instead of leaving mental and emotional balance to chance or mood, all of us can learn and practice simple strategies to keep ourselves centered. Like exercise routines for keeping our bodies fit, these mental practices will build our "inner fitness" so that even while engaged in a grueling task or experiencing a day when everything seems to go wrong, we can maintain a calm and untroubled focus.

Mind Like Water offers busy people a set of specific tools for maintaining a state of balance and perspective from which to respond to changing events. The book presents strategies for keeping the mind focused, the attention centered, and the emotions under control—all this while in the very act of addressing problems and making decisions in a world where uncertainty rules. Using these easy-to-use, grab-and-go techniques, readers learn to connect with their inner gyroscopes and remain quietly poised while all around them is rush and clangor and worry. *Mind Like Water* is a book about how to live in a crazy world without participating in its craziness.

As many readers will know, the term "mind like water" is far from original with me. It is an ancient Zen concept. In the philosophy of Taoism, the original Chinese way of liberation that combined with Indian Buddhism to produce Zen, the goal is to realize the Tao, and the way is to develop mind like water. As Alan Watts writes in *The Way of Zen,* "So long as the conscious intellect is frantically trying to clutch the world in its net of abstractions, and to insist that life be bound and fitted to its rigid categories, the mood of Taoism will remain incomprehensible, and the intellect will wear itself out."

One arena in which many human minds are wearing themselves out these days is that of decision-making. Using Mind Like Water instead of the intellect, it is possible to arrive at decisions spontaneously. This is accomplished by letting the mind alone, trusting it to work by itself. The Taoist reserves the term "non-grasping" to describe the mind functioning in this way. "The perfect man employs his mind as a mirror. It grasps nothing; it refuses nothing. It receives, but does not keep." With this total absence of mental straining and striving, a clarity is reached that is unachievable by the rational intellectual process.

As Westerners we are used to separating science and the mind. Even psychology, which comes close to being considered a science, has been formulated as an observation and study of mental, emotional, and behavioral phenomena rather than as a discipline of deliberate self-scrutiny and self-change. The word *noetics* (from the Greek *nous,* meaning mind or ways of knowing) better describes what this book is about. Acknowledging mind and consciousness as the roots of human experience, noetics is concerned with transforming one's experience by deliberately and continously changing the way people see things. This book takes you on a journey of tinkering with your own ideas, deliberately challenging your assumptions, and ultimately changing your experience by changing your mind.

What Is Mind Like Water?

All creatures have an intimate, life-sustaining relationship with water. Our planet was once covered with it, so we all came from it.

Humans spend their nine-month prenatal period suspended in it. Beyond our need of water for all of the basic routines of drinking, cooking, bathing, washing, and growing things, we humans have an elemental need to be around water. There's something about water that gives us back to ourselves. Its appearance, its sound, its very feel sustain us mentally and emotionally. Whether as thundering cataracts, rolling breakers, trickling streams, pattering rains, or rippleless, star-mirroring depths, water has the power to instill awe, induce calmness, and inspire reflection.

Each summer we head for lakes and beaches, seeking recovery from the dryness of daily routines. During the long winter months many of us induce relief artificially by placing little trickling waterfalls in our workrooms, or playing recordings of gentle surfs, or gazing at pictures of seascapes.

Watermind

Over the centuries human beings have seen in the nature of water a metaphor for right behavior. Calmness and fluidity have always been considered essential to highest athletic performance and artistic endeavor. Recognizing that certain properties of water depict the actions and attitudes of people who are thinking and operating at their best, Zen masters and martial arts instructors have sought to help their students achieve a mental state they call "mind like water."

Even today, when we want to describe the experience of effortlessly transcending stress and strain, we speak of "being in the flow." That exhilarating sense of being in the right place at the right time is analogous to what athletes call being *in the zone,* a state in which the mind spins free, all stress and strain disappears, and activity becomes effortless. The constant turbulence in which we live and work has its downside; it trains our minds to be constantly on the go, with the result that we are stressed and restless even when we have opportunity to be less so. This problem requires us to seek ways to balance ourselves, to be calm and purposeful instead of driven and impatient. By adopting these same characteristics of fluidity and grace, we cultivate the ability to enter that sublime zone where time stops and we are free to move around in the moment in joy.

I have chosen the term *aquanamous* as an occasional substitute for the phrase "mind like water"—the goal to be attained through practices presented in this book. The aquanamous mind can be likened to that freedom of perception described by Lao Tzu as apprehension of the Tao. The term is analogous to *cosmic consciousness* (Bucke and others), to *wu wei* as presented in Zen Buddhism, to *grokking* (Heinlein), to *samadhi* (Hindu), and to *nirvana* (Buddha). Most of these terms have been regarded by Westerners as beyond their own possibility of attaining the mysterious psychical realm occupied only by masters and gurus. That it is possible to actually practice everyday methods that move one toward attaining these states comes to many as a shock.

Aquanamous Attributes

What exactly does it mean to have a mind like water? We can induce the answer by reviewing some of the properties of water and applying them to our hearts and minds. Consider each of the following in terms of the mind. There is water's fluidity, the ability to flow around things easily. Absorption, the taking in of anything thrown into it. Reflection, the perfect mirroring of things. There is implacability, the relentless wearing down of hard objects. Motivelessness, proceeding on its way toward a goal of balance without frustration or dismay. Finally, essence, water's ability to simply be itself regardless of its changing form.

Surely these qualities of water represent worthy goals for busy people in this turbulent world. But they do not come easily to our speed-addicted society. They require daily practice of stillness and reflection. Underlying all is a major assumption:

> *Changing your mind is the most powerful step you can take toward altering your world.*

This book is divided into eight parts: "Fluidity," "Level-Seeking," "Reflection," "Absorption," "Form-Changing," "Motivelessness," "Implacability," and "Essence." Each part applies a particular attribute of water to the mind and furnishes three key steps to follow to help in developing the mental equivalent of that water characteristic. The book's twenty-four progressive steps can be thought of as something like a series of weight machines ranged around the space of an inner gymnasium. By performing mental calisthenics on one or more of these mechanisms each day, the reader can build strength in a particular noetic area toward the desired end state: a Mind like Water.

You are invited to start now to develop an inner fitness that allows you to access inner states of happiness and calmness that are already within you, an integration of mind and body that frees you from stress and worry. With your continuing practice of each of the twenty-four steps that follow, you will find yourself taking charge of your responses to outer changes and setbacks until, in the words of Paramahansa Yogananda speaking of the benefits of meditation, you will be able to "stand unshaken amid the crash of breaking worlds."

fluidity

◈

Water runs no faster or slower than is called for. Its flow is even, unforced, liquidity itself. Naturally and without effort, it always seeks its own level.

Lesson: Stay in the moment. Don't hurry, don't stop. Listen to yourself, and never be rushed.

Trust Your Intuition

The greatest problems in life can never be solved. They must be out-grown, by attaining a new level of consciousness.

—CARL GUSTAV JUNG

Years ago I conducted a week-long seminar for the staff of a government school for Navajo children in Arizona. During my morning runs over the desert, I would sometimes see an old Native American man, tall and erect, striding swiftly along a road or a trail. Something about his one-pointed concentration and the powerful way he walked drew my attention. With his old clothes, faded red headband, and his long white hair streaming out behind him, he seemed the very image of a patriarch.

I described the old man to one of the teachers in my seminar group. "That's Charley Good Horse," he said. "There are lots of stories about him." When I asked my friend to share one, he told me the following anecdote:

Once my brother-in-law Henry was driving his pickup to town along a deserted road, and he came across Charley walking along. He stopped and asked the old man if he wanted a lift.

"No, thanks, I'm in a hurry," Charley said.

Henry didn't know what to make of that, but he drove ahead. A mile or so down the road one of the truck tires blew out. He got out to change it, only to find that his spare was flat. He sat down and waited. Pretty soon here came Charley, striding along. He walked past Henry without a word or a glance, and on out of sight.

Later a friend came along and gave my brother-in-law a ride into town. Of course, Charley Good Horse had reached there long ago and was gone.

How did the old man know to refuse the offer of a ride? How did he know he would save time by walking? Presumably he was relying on *inner knowing*—the ability to know a thing completely and all at once, without relying on sensory data. If we could train this inner knowing, what a strategic advantage we would gain in a world of everyday confusion and unpredictability! We could size up a new situation right away and assess its possibilities. We could know immediately whether to trust a new person or situation. When others were confused by a sudden, unexpected turn of events, we could use it to advantage. We could avoid going down every wrong path. We could make speedy decisions that always turn out right.

Nature of Intuition

When it comes to intuition, there's good news and there's bad news. The good news is, we all possess the capacity for inner knowing. Intuition is not something outside us that must be added to our makeup as humans. We come equipped with this powerful capacity; it is a sleeping giant, a hidden source of wisdom just waiting to be tapped. The bad news is, most of us were raised on another planet than the one that sponsored Charley Good Horse. Intuition is like a muscle that has atrophied through nonuse. Each of us must train the intuition muscle to athletic performance. Most

of us have spent all or most of our time relying on rational inference, and in the process denied our intuitive faculty. So we have
two problems. We don't quite know how to believe in our inner
knowing, and we've grown so busy listening to our mental ma-
chinery processing sensory data that we don't know how to shut
out its demanding clamor.

What is intuition? Paramahansa Yogananda, the author of the
spiritual classic *Autobiography of a Yogi,* defined intuition as "that
directly perceiving faculty of the soul that at once knows the truth
about anything, requiring no medium of sense experience or reason. It does not consist in believing a thing, but in knowing it directly and unmistakably. It does not contradict. It is always
supported by a right sense of perception, reason, and inference, although it does not depend upon any data whatsoever offered by
the senses or the mind. A real intuition can never be wrong.
Everyone possesses this quality more or less. Like any faculty, it
must be cultivated."

That last phrase—"it must be cultivated"—is the kicker. Most
of us have formed a lifelong habit of relying on only one way of
knowing—drawing conclusions from information brought to us by
our senses. This overuse of the intellect has conditioned us to fear
or mistrust other ways of knowing. Building the intuition muscle is
an investment; it takes time, but in the end it will save much time.
Like any long-term learning it requires skill and practice, but it offers undreamed-of possibilities as returns on the investment.

A Personal Story

One morning shortly after I had moved back to the West Coast in
1979 I found myself running along a path at the top of a cliff
above the Pacific Ocean in Encinitas, California. It was dark, just
before dawn, and the sea wall was deserted; only an occasional
light glimmering far out to sea rivaled the stars. Feeling the off-
shore breeze against my face and bare legs, listening to the waves

crashing against the rocks below, I exulted in the freshness and the beauty around me. My running body was a part of a harmonious whole, a panoramic orchestration heralding a beautiful morning.

Then I seemed to hear a whisper coming from inside my body. It formed into a pair of meaningless but mellifluous-sounding syllables in my mind, which gradually grew into a chant. To the beat of my running steps I gave voice to it, feeling a bursting joy: *Kahlee! . . . Kah-lee!* Somehow I knew that it was good and right for me to be doing this. Several months later, a friend gave me a copy of Paramahansa Yogananda's *Autobiography of a Yogi*. A few pages into the text, reading the author's account of his early life in India, I came across these words: "Our family moved to Lahore in the Punjab. There I acquired a picture of the Divine Mother in the form of the Goddess Kali."

I was stunned. No wonder on that morning run I had felt such an abounding bliss on that seacliff run—I had been chanting the name of a Nature god! I later learned that on that morning I had been a few hundred yards from the seaside ashram that Yogananda occupied for many years. Many mysterious experiences led me eventually to the feet of this master, who had left his body in 1952.

It Will Be *Done*

Vernon Kitabu Turner, a martial arts instructor and spiritual teacher, carries the matter of trust beyond the processing of information altogether. As a young boy growing up in the projects, Turner was often taunted by neighborhood bullies for his introspective nature and quiet pursuits. He vowed to become a protector of himself and others, and he prayed for help. He says: "Now when you take that spiritual path, the action does not come from you. I remember the first time I became aware that my body could move but that I wasn't moving it because when a person threw a punch, my hand blocked it and threw them, and I didn't even *know* that move. And then as I began to let go more and more, I found out that the mastery was already there; I just had to get out of the way to let it emerge, to show itself."

The Japanese have the word *mushin,* by which they mean "the art of no-mind." That's when there is no conscious attempt to act, and yet you move anyway, when the action comes from such a deep place that there is no one to take credit for it. In this chaotic, unpredictable world, there is a great need for all of us to learn how to live that way. Can we find a state of trust and calmness wherein we perceive that action arises not from us, but through us, independently of our control? Can it perhaps be as the Bible says— that we need "take no thought for the morrow"?

Mind Like Water Exercises

■ *Feel the Force*
Whenever you can, in moments during routine work consciously feel that it is not you, but the energy of life force coming through you, that is doing the work. Visualize this force pouring through your mind and muscles, and practice getting out of its way.

■ *Adopt the Art of No-Mind*
Practice not knowing ahead of time what will happen or what you will do. Enter each moment merely resolved to do what needs to be done, merely noticing when the moves—computer keystrokes, verbal responses to customers, packing product, contributing in a team meeting—emerge.

■ *Use "It Will Be Done"*
When in your workday you find you are fussing ("What am I gonna *do?*"), see what happens when you say, "I'm not worried about it. I don't have to do anything. It will be *done.*" Stay alert, let go, watch for the solution to be given—even if it's at the last moment.

■ *Play the Observer*

See what happens if you clear your mind and allow yourself to do exactly what is necessary, exactly what is correct, with exquisite, one-pointed concentration. When it's all over with, see if you don't feel that you've observed more than you've participated.

■ *Paddle on the Crest*

World-class whitewater kayakers don't fight the flow, they cooperate with it. The only time they dip the paddle is to right the boat or keep it headed downstream; the rest of the time they relax and enjoy the ride. When you're in the trough of a wave and boat ends are in the water, it's useless to paddle; you can't make any lateral movement. The rule is: *Dip on the crest.* Wait until the boat ends are out and you can see; then a slight dip of the paddle gives the boat the required directional correction.

It's so in life. When we're in the trough—that is, mired in change, can't see where we're going, feeling anxious—we can exhaust ourselves by flailing about in worry, trying different schemes, etc., and make absolutely no difference. Waiting is hard but necessary. Relax, take stock, organize, get little things done. Then when the crest comes, you can see where you're going, and every stroke counts exponentially.

■ *Look for Opportunities*

Cooperating with the swirling tempo of change instead of fighting it involves a whole new way of observing things. Instead of being set back by surprises, lean into them. Look for them expectantly, and when one comes, carefully assess its value—look past the danger to the opportunities it offers. Between the waves of change lies the hidden window. When you see it flash, act trustfully and decisively. Seeing without prejudice is the key to participating skillfully in a world of change.

■ *Loosen Your Hold on Your Preferences*

By clinging to your habits and preferences you may be hiding precious hidden meanings from yourself. Pause and look again. With eyes unjaded and unsophisticated, you may glimpse whole new treasures. The *Dhammapada,* a traditional Zen work, says:

If you want The Great Way to appear before your eyes,
Cherish neither "for" nor "against."
To compare what you like with what you dislike,
That is the disease of the mind.
Then you pass over the hidden meaning;
Peace of mind is needlessly troubled.

■ Read the Future in the Past and the Present

Most people fail to recognize the link between their fixing on what is current, and their inability to cope with change. In America we are fascinated with events. The media feed the popular obsession with what's-hot-and-what's-not. For us to get above our harmful myopia, a more intuitive approach is needed—actually, a way to predict the future. With proper vision, you can do this. First, lift your perspective above events. Try to recognize broader reaches of time and activity. Once you see a repeating pattern, extrapolate and predict what will come next. It's fun to see what you predicted come to pass.

■ Gain Perspective by Hindsight

Practice of the Mind Like Water state allows us to see that what appears to be a disaster is simply the next thing that is happening. Instead of being incapacitated with panic, the mind rises above and assesses the entire picture, taking no action until it has considered that this "bad" thing may be a good thing in disguise. Trouble can be felicity in disguise. (Sometimes the disguise is perfect!) Look back at an event that you experienced as a disaster at the time. Think: "If that hadn't happened, I would not be/do/have _____ today." Fill in the blank with somebody you met, a new skill or trait you acquired, a new direction you took, a job or career you began as a result of that episode. Then crank the time window forward to the present.

Meet setbacks by "looking back at them from the future," imagining what gifts they'll bring in time. When something bad happens, ask yourself, What possible benefits will ensue as a result of this painful event? What will I be telling myself about it in five years? Ten? Will it seem like a bad thing then?

For many of us, developing intuition requires a suspension of disbelief. When we are working with our beliefs, it's a little bit like rewiring an old house. The present outmoded wiring must stay in for a while to run the house as the new circuits are being implanted. As work proceeds, care must be taken to avoid costly accidents, overloads, or blowouts from the old faulty wiring. Finally comes the day when the old system has been completely replaced, and the upgrade kicks in once and for all.

STEP 2

Live in the Moment

Live for the day only, and for the day's work. The chief worries of life arise from the foolish habit of looking before and after.

—Sir William Oslet

People spend much of their lives futurizing, and thereby rob themselves of their native aliveness, self-expression, and joy. What I call futurizing is not to be confused with the normal and quite necessary process of looking ahead—making plans, setting goals, keeping schedules, and being at places on time. It's by being so concerned with *what's next* that we steal attention from the present, the only place where our power and our joy can be accessed. Futurizing is the ultimate absent-mindedness. When the mind becomes focused exclusively on the future, pretty soon we're not *here* at all.

Our strength, our joy, our creativity are always experienced in some moment of Now. Unless we enter the moment, these powers are lost to us. We cannot gain them by thinking about them or imagining them; we must *experience* them. The more you learn to live in the Now, the stronger and smarter and happier you will be. Operating on a moment-to-moment basis with quietness of mind, you build up a reserve of healthy functioning. When setbacks occur, that reserve enables you to navigate through the difficulties with the same peacefulness and alertness you have been practicing all along.

In their groundbreaking book *Slowing Down to the Speed of Life,* Richard Carlson and Joseph Bailey depict mental health as an already existing state in each of us, rather than something to be achieved and maintained. What can we do to access this health that lives within us? They write: "The entry point for mental health is living in the moment. In order to understand how to live in the moment, we need to understand how we create our psychological experience of life. Our experience comes from our thinking, and thinking, when combined with consciousness, gives us the experience of our reality."

Knowing that our thinking creates our experience helps us to disidentify with it. By using what these authors call *thought recognition* we can wake up to the fact "I am feeling this way because I am thinking this way." This automatically changes our thinking and places us back where we belong: in the Now. To get an idea of where you have tended to spend most of your life (i.e., your thinking), try the following exercise.

Looking Down on Your Life

Imagine you are taking an aerial view of the past two or three years of your life. As you gaze down on that spread-out span of time, can you see the little figure that was you? Can you watch its running through so many moments and hours and days of that time, streaking through time like its hair was on fire? Where were you going in such a hurry? What was the rush? More importantly, what was the outcome of it all? Can you look into that person's mind and find that much of the time he or she was not being with what was happening at the moment, because of being so concerned with what was coming *next?*

Futurizing perpetuates itself. If you've been running all that time, it's likely you're still running. All that time you spent trying to be up in some imagined future time, you were training yourself *not to be here now!* Imagine your life continuing in this rushing fashion. Is it possible that one day you'll be looking back and lamenting, "A lot of good things happened in my life, but I was never around to enjoy them!"

Eckhart Tolle, author of the extraordinary book *The Power of Now,* writes: "When you are on a journey, it is certainly helpful to know where you are going or at least the general direction in which you are moving, but don't forget: the only thing that is ultimately real about your journey is the step that you are taking at this moment. That's all there ever is. Your life's journey has an outer purpose and an inner purpose.... The outer purpose belongs to the horizontal dimension of space and time; the inner purpose concerns a deepening of your Being in the vertical dimension of the timeless Now. Your outer journey may contain a million steps; your inner journey only has one: the step you are taking right now. As you become more deeply aware of this one step, you realize that it already contains within itself all the other steps, as well as the destination."

Benefits of Living in the Moment

- Efficiency
  Businesspeople take pains to eliminate unnecessary steps, cut costs, find the best deal, etc. When they recognize that an activity has absolutely no benefit and incurs substantial costs, they throw it out. If you are in the business of living more efficiently, you need to eliminate—expunge, utterly obliterate—the activity of worry. Forget about what might,

did, could, or should happen. Consider this saying: "Worry is like interest paid on a debt that never comes due."

- Fearlessness
Extreme-sports athletes tell us that fear and present-moment-consciousness can't coexist. Being here now gives you ease and confidence, no matter what storm is going on around you. A wise person said, "Worry is fear of the future. Guilt is fear of the past. If we stay in the present, we will have no fear."

- Total Intelligence
Being in the moment doesn't mean being spaced-out, mindless; it means being totally mind*ful*. When you are fully in the moment you are intellectually, emotionally, and spiritually available.

- Creativity
"Wherever you go, there you are." When you are fully present, you operate outside of time. The present is the only place where something can be created. New solutions come from a change of heart, from seeing life differently. This happens when you enter the Flow.

- Influence
When you come to the moment and live in the moment, people around you automatically experience your aliveness and spontaneity, and want to follow your example.

Mind Like Water Exercises

- *Decide Where You'll Live*
Maybe living in the future is not something you want to give up. There are payoffs for any addiction, but they're all short-term. In-

evitably, after the high comes the low. If you want to come home to the moment, make a commitment. Do it.

■ *Stop in Your Tracks*

Try it now. It might be hard. (The mind goes, "Stop? STOP?? You gotta be kidding! I can't *stop!* If you knew all the things I have to do, etc.") Try it anyway. Fake it, if need be, just so you can enter the place you've been avoiding—that portal of terror with the sign over the door saying HERE AND NOW.

■ *Come Home*

Home is where they have to take you in. That's the Present. Right now, put things out of your hands. Uncross your arms and legs. Sit back. Relax. Close your eyes. Take a breath. Feel the air on your skin. Feel your scalp. Feel your toes. Watch your breath. Listen to your heart; catch it doing things right—one measured beat at a time.

■ *Expand Time*

Think of what it's like when time goes away for you; that's when you are truly in the present. Was it when you fell in love? Or discovered a great intellectual concept? Or communed with the natural world? Or engaged with your Higher Power? Concentrating on the memory of a higher state of consciousness can induce it to visit again. Dwell on and analyze those times, and try to recapture that same feeling. When you live in the present, you expand time.

■ *Go by Body Time*

As a kid you didn't live by clock time, you lived by body time. Time wasn't chopped up into little pieces and run by a tick-tock machine; it was a broad expanse to move around in. Every day you went out to play was a fresh adventure where everything presented to your senses was a gift. (That's why it's called the "present.") Live that way now. Get back to body time.

■ *Set It and Forget It*

We worry about forgetting things—and then actually forget them! Why? It's because when we operate in a habitually stressed-out state of mind, only a small part of our intelligence can squeeze through the crack. Relax and remember. When you look at a piece of data, focus on it, place it where you'll find it, and forget it. Trust your intuition to summon the information you need, when you need it. You'll not only keep appointments, you'll also arrive mentally alive.

■ *Don't Hurry, Don't Stop*

Go about your activities in a "calmly active, actively calm" attitude, watching to pick up clues that things are unfolding around you as if by a hidden plan. Consciously, inside yourself, seek to find in each moment the clues that will tell you how to play your part in this story.

■ *Live an Adventure*

An adventure is when you don't know what will happen but you have to go to find out. Try living today—or even a few hours of it—as an adventure. Don't know what will happen until it happens.

When you return full attention to the moment you're in, you conquer time, and learn why real time exists only in the Now. The present is infinite—it's timeless. Only what happens in the present, counts. The present is the only place you can experience Joy. Happiness can come true for you at any second, with awareness. It's in this moment. Unless your mind has been so future-trained that you avoid it, you will feel a trickling-up of Joy. Why does Joy—capital-J Joy, Joy for no reason—live in the present moment? Because when you come to the present, you rejoin your Self. You *are* that unconditioned Joy. When you feel the Joy you are, the old "If only I had _____, I'd be happy" routine is reduced to foolishness. Only when you are fully present can you see clearly the right thing to do. You are in touch with your Self, and the right thing to do is doing right by your Self.

This is the day the Lord hath made;
let us be glad and rejoice in it.

—Psalm 118:24

STEP 3

Keep the Instrument Tuned

There has never been and never will be again the combination of molecules and atoms that is you. Your job in the world is to live out that potential.

—ANONYMOUS

A sound mind is supported by a sound body. Development of Mind Like Water is difficult if not impossible to achieve if you are violating the pure and pristine state in which your physical form is meant to operate. Proper diet, nutrition, and regular exercise contribute to a mind that can free itself into the moment and operate at peak efficiency.

A frequent saying in metaphysical circles is "We are not bodies that have souls, but rather souls that have bodies." We are not humans having a spiritual experience, but spirits having a human experience. Who you are is the essence; your body is the form that essence is temporarily taking. The functions and relative importance of the human body are placed in perspective when we consider the concept of reincarnation, the taking up of a succession of

forms by the elemental soul. If each of us has been men and
women of every race and clime, and will continue to be so, then
this body may be seen to be only a temporary vehicle for occupy-
ing this present go-round of existence.

The headlong race of daily routines that someone has named the
"dailython" is tailor-made for our losing touch with our spiritual nature. It is the program that keeps delusion in place, convincing us
from the time we open our eyes each morning that we *are* our bodies, our ages, our weight and height, our families and jobs, our area
codes and zip codes. When we look in the mirror we think, *This is
me.* Wrong. In Mind Like Water we exchange that limiting cocoon
of body mentality for the vastness of Self-realization.

The Body as Instrument

What is your body? It is your instrument for expressing yourself.
Think of a fine musical instrument, upon which the owner plays
for long hours at a time. Maintaining that mechanism in top condition, keeping it finely tuned, treating it with special care must be
top priorities. There is another reason to carefully maintain the
body; it is a vehicle, your means of getting around in the world. In
both realms of your physical functioning, instrumental and vehic-
ular, a properly balanced attitude is key. On the one hand, you
must pay attention to your body to keep it in good running
order—diet, nutrition, sleep, fitness, etc. On the other, it is good to
heed what Eastern sages mean when they say "Give the body its
due, no more." Placing too much emphasis and attention on the
physical simply returns one to a false identification with it.

Each person owes the constant tuning and maintenance of his
or her body instrument not only to self but also to environment,
loved ones, and community. Why are you obliged to care for your
body? It is because no one else can be found who can play exactly
your tune. Care of your body is one way you can appreciate your
own uniqueness. It is an everyday means of affirming that there is

something good about being you as yourself. The body, your instrument, is a means of finding your voice and expressing the song you came into the world to sing. You must not die with the symphony of your life unfinished.

Tuning Up

I began running at a time when it was uncommon to see runners on streets or along country roads. Those were days when motorists gawked (and sometimes yelled or dared me off into the gutter). As the fitness boom hit in the late seventies, people I met who knew that I ran would often ask, "How far do you run?" To this I always replied, "I don't know." As this response was inconceivable to askers, other questions would follow: How long did I run? How fast? Always the answer was the same: I didn't know. It was true. I didn't *care* to know. My running was never about scorekeeping. It was a mind laboratory I'd stumbled upon, a means of taking myself away into a place of dreaming. Like other runners, I enjoyed the blissful rush when the endorphins—the pleasure-making chemicals of the brain—kicked in after a few miles. But running was primarily a place for me to explore my ideas, beliefs, and perceptions, to stand outside of business-as-usual and see what else there was. In other words, running was my introduction to meditation.

Time is the slave driver of most people when they work out. Private exercise is dominated by recordkeeping: scores, averages, times, miles, all ruled by scorecards, stopwatches, speedometers, exercise machine meters, and bathroom scales. Exercisers with their mind on numbers—so many repetitions, so much time elapsed, so many miles run, certain heart rate achieved, so many pounds lost—must treat the body as a beast of burden.

When exercise has value only as it contributes to some future point in time, the power of the present moment cannot be felt, played with, or blissfully enjoyed. Watching the clock makes the workout routine even more of a drudgery, a duty, and an obligation.

Done this way, exercise is not a release from the daily battle of life, it's just more of it.

Often I have the feeling during a task or an activity that it is not me doing the doing but that it is being done through me with my cooperation. I call this sensation Being Run. The Being Run experience transforms the experience of exercise, making it enjoyable and infinitely rewarding beyond any goal of mere time or space. Being Run is the real seat of joy in exercising; it is the body feeling itself being sung through by the Life Force.

Mind Like Water Exercises

■ *Appreciate the Body*

Look at yourself in the mirror—at your hair, your teeth, your eyes, your complexion—and see that they all belong there, and that you belong there, as you are. Realize that you have a perfect right to be in this universe, to be this way, and you see that there is a basic hospitality that this world provides to you. You have looked and you have seen, and you don't have to apologize for being born on this earth.

The body that belongs to you is not just one of many; it deserves the respect and care due any one-of-a-kind model. The hawking media relentlessly parade examples of the current fashion of looks and physique, inviting gullible viewers to compare their appearances with those models and try to emulate them through diet, cosmetics, muscle-building, and even surgery.

Why should what others think is beautiful or stylish have anything to do with the way you feel about yourself physically? It is a travesty to compare your body with any other. Appreciate the elemental purity of your body, an instrument divinely constructed, designed by a Master to be flawless in its functioning. In its own blessed right, your body may be said to be a Stradivarius of physiques. You are absolutely one of a kind—unprecedented and unrepeatable. Out of all the combinations that might have occurred, against the odds of millions to one, one egg and one sperm united to conceive—you.

■ *Affirm the Self*
Loosen your mind's hold on its identification with the body. Relax and affirm:

> I am changeless, timeless, weightless. I am the immortal soul. I have come on earth for this little time to entertain and be entertained. As I behold the tragedies and comedies of this changeable life, I will remember Who I Really Am—a child of the Eternal, playing on the lap of Omnipresence.

■ *Appreciate the Body's Changes*
There are two periods in our earthly round—early life and old age—when the following are more or less true:

- Time does not mean much.
- You are fascinated by the obvious.
- You live in the present.
- What others think of you doesn't matter.
- Life is a continual adventure.

When you compare these characteristics with the mentality of the middle part of life, in which there is so much of running either away from or after something, which time seems to make more sense? In a society obsessed with youth, we need a new understanding of aging, one that honors the aging process as a teacher. We have only to look at those who have made great contributions to the world in letters, arts, government, and science to realize that often a great contributor's actual body of work does not begin to show up until he or she is over forty. However, the aging process in this country has a bad rap; rather than a rich harvesting of the rewards of life's lessons and experience, it is viewed as a time of debilitation and loss of energies and faculties.

When old age is regarded as a clinical problem, it is difficult to look consciously at our own aging, at our parents' aging—indeed, at the needs of the largest population of aged people in human history. Instead of succumbing to modern America's stereotypic vision of aging—fearing the changes in our bodies, resisting the natural transitions of life, avoiding the unknown territory of death—we need to open ourselves to receiving the gifts of age: mature perspective, seasoned creativity, and spiritual vision.

More reliable and instructional than educating ourselves through sensational reporting of news through newspapers and television is the actual experience of aging, of being able to look back over many decades with a heightened perspective and an appreciation of the evanescent here-and-now. Being older means you can see through the ruckus; breathe easily when the sky is falling; and, best of all, look not outward but within the mind for your happiness.

■ *Don't Just Age ... Sage*

Appreciate the aging of your body; never fear it. Know always that the best is yet to come. All of us, at whatever age we are, are growing old. Do we need to experience a diminution of powers in the process? Hardly. We are meant to grow wiser and happier at each stage of life. The notion of *saging,* instead of just aging, was contributed by Rabbi Zalman Schacter. It means to regard the aging process as a time of being more in touch with your capacities, more joyfully aware of the particular path you were meant to tread, more open-heartedly contributing to the world in your own unique ways, and less concerned with what others think. You have become an expert in *you*-ness. Now use it and enjoy it.

■ *Relive Your Childhood*

It is never too late to have a happy childhood. One of my most appreciated changes through my sixties has been recurring moments of time recaptured. I am fascinated by occasional flashbacks to my youth. These are not mere memories, but re-created epiphanies. The green light of our front lawn on a summer morning. The sound of peepers from a nearby brook in the spring night. A sense of being followed home through the deep snow on a winter's evening after a hard day of play by a great, overshadowing Presence. Where do these pictures come from? The brain is somehow freed at this point in life to pull old files never before reviewed, snapshots imbued with the Life Force, re-creations of the very feeling of being alive in that moment.

■ Listen for the Voice

During all those years when I was inhaling my rations as if they would disappear from my plate, I was disregarding a subtle signal, with the result that I often indulged in overeating. Nowadays, if I go slowly, I can sense inside myself precisely when a certain point is reached—the silent sound of my body's intuitive inner Voice— and stop the intake. The silent cue comes several clicks short of fullness, allowing the last few mouthfuls to settle into the stomach comfortably, with no sense of surfeit. Throughout life I obeyed my mother's rule to clean the plate. Now it's a point of pride to leave some food on it.

■ Go for a Dream Walk

As you run, walk, or perform some other physical exercise, induce the feeling that you are "being run," by using one or another of the following mental methods:

Breath pull	Imagine that it's not your will or muscles, but that your inhaling is pulling you forward.
Tow rope	Pretend there is an invisible rope, attached to your chest, that is gently pulling you forward.
Giant hand	Imagine a giant hand resting against your back, gently pushing you along.
Conveyor belt	Concentrate on the path ahead of you, and imagine the path is moving instead of you.

Frames Imagine that you are in a motion picture. You are moving merely to occupy future "frames."

These and similar techniques may be found in my book *What's the Rush?*

Physically speaking, barring abnormal difficulties we come into the world just about the best that Life can make us. The capacity for bursting health, mental acuity, and emotional well-being, as well as vitality and intense pleasure, are built into the body-mind instrument. It is our ideas and habits that limit us and make us ill. Mind Like Water is consistent with care of our instruments. The Being Run experience offers a mental vacation from all the other goal-dominated parts of life. Instead of times and distances, it deals in the cranking up of joy in the momentary wonder of being alive. That joy is the joy of the soul translating through the body, through a relishing of bodily sensations, a pleasuring of nerves and muscles, a reveling in physical energy and vitality. When participated in fully and regularly, Being Run spills its effortless validity, its sheer enjoyment of the moment of Now, into the rest of life. It offers a cure for the anxious sense of rush, the overpowering need to *get there* that pervades common life today.

level-seeking

❧

Water flows ever from higher to lower,
seeking its own level.
If it is unbalanced, it flows until its force
achieves harmony again.

*Lesson: Seek equilibrium in your life.
Teach yourself to respond instinctively
whenever you are out of balance.*

STEP 4

Balance Control with Surrender

Life is what happens when you're making other plans.

—MODERN SAYING

One of the secrets of living successfully in a crazy world is to find the balance between *making* things happen and *letting* things happen. Often in their quest for success people emphasize aggressiveness and control to such an extent that it is difficult for them to take the pressure off—or even to imagine a reason to do so. When it comes to preserving balance and perspective, though, overcontrol can be a liability.

Great leaders know about surrender as they know about control; with them it's all a matter of timing. Like whitewater paddlers, as change speeds up they know when to dip the paddle and when to enjoy the ride. Most importantly, their momentary balance between the control and the surrender forces enables them to use the divining rod of intuition to discern answers perfectly and immediately—without necessarily knowing how they know them. They are not looking at things, they are *feeling* them from within, with instant, effortless understanding. They're transcending the hurry-up. They're making more time.

Through exquisite management of attention, any person can begin to train his or her balance and intuitive functioning like an athlete. Information from sports figures about being "in the zone" can enrich us, connecting that extraordinary functioning with our own experience. For example, Bill Russell of the Boston Celtics—the team that won eleven national championships in thirteen years—described the experience of perfect attention and response this way:

> Every so often a Celtic game would heat up so that it became magical. When it happened, I could feel my play rise to a new level. Three or four plays were not enough to get it going. It would surround not only me and the other Celtics, but also the players on the other team and even the referees. At that special level, all sorts of odd things happened. The game would be in a white heat of competititon—which is a miracle in itself—yet I never felt the pain. The game would be surprising, yet nothing could surprise me. It was almost as if we were playing in slow motion. I could almost sense how the next play would develop and where the next shot would be taken. Even before the other team brought the ball in bounds, I could feel it so keenly that I'd want to shout to my teammates, "It's coming there!" except that that I knew that everything would change if I did. My premonitions would be consistently correct, and I always felt then that I not only knew all the Celtics by heart, but also all the opposing players, and that they all knew me. These were moments when I had chills pulsing up and down my spine. Sometimes the feeling would last all the way to the end of the game. On the occasions when the game ended at that special level, I literally did not care who had won. If we lost, I'd still be as free and as high as a skyhawk.

Though we're not aware of it, our habits are an everyday way of experiencing being on automatic pilot. Actually, your habits have been doing the work you thought you were doing, ever since you woke up this morning. You did not have to learn all over again how to walk or speak or eat or drive your car; you did these things routinely, likely while thinking about something else. Realize now, by pausing momentarily between the busy moments of the day, that *your work is doing you.* Stand aside from it, and see the action arising from the same force that animates your bodily systems and cognitive processes. Relax, and feel that force using your mind and body to get work done. In this way you can learn to *let* many things happen, not just *make* them happen. The balance between *letting* and *making* can bring relaxation, comfort, even blissfulness into your work.

Something of the experience Bill Russell describes can come in any endeavor, on any day, to the intuitively tuned player. It's not hard to imagine, because we've all tuned in at times to a day at work that seems almost magical. We feel our play rise to a new level. Things seem almost to be moving in slow motion, giving us all the time in the world to do what we need to do. Nothing surprises us or sets us back. We can sense what will develop before it happens, then watch our premonitions play out. In an extraordinary way we are tuned in to the environment—our own people, the competition, customers. We seem to know them all by heart, and to be known by them. In this heightened consciousness we don't care about who gets the credit. We're not keeping score. However the game comes out, we will have benefited. We are "as free and as high as a skyhawk."

These experiences teach us that we already have the intuitive capacity to "play out of our heads." How can we develop this inner edge so as to use it more often? How can we find the right balance between *making* things happen and *letting* them happen? Following is a simple exercise that may help you discover more balance right where you live. To do it, you need an "item"—a current problem you are facing, or an area where you are experiencing dissatisfaction.

The Control vs. Surrender Activity

1. Write down a description of the item in one short phrase.

2. Sit quietly alone, spine erect, feet flat on the floor. Relax, and close your eyes. Spend thirty seconds concentrating on the issue you wrote down. Then let it go.

3. Become aware of your breathing without changing it. Concentrate on it to the exclusion of all thoughts. Observe it as if it is that of another person.

4. Alternate several fifteen-second periods of breathing with "being breathed." In the latter case, called Surrender Breathing, pretend the air is breathing you. You are a vessel, into which the air is alternately pushing, and drawing itself out. Then return to Control Breathing, where you perceive yourself clearly as the breather. Switch back and forth several times, studying the feelings associated with each kind of perception, until you have identified them.

5. Open your eyes and write down the words "control" and "surrender." Under each, list the feelings or attitudes you connected with each kind of breathing you practiced.

6. Now look back at your item. Identify which list of feelings connects more strongly with the way you have been addressing the problem you noted in step 1.

Consider practicing the other kind of approach.
If you have been trying to control the problem, ask:

- What advantages might it bring?
- What does it have to teach me?
- How can I leverage it or cooperate with it?

If you have been surrendering to the problem, ask:

- What resources could I marshal for an attack?
- Who could I tell or ask about it?
- What are the steps of an action plan?

Life is not all control, nor is it all surrender. It is best lived with an eye on the moment, and with the will poised to act when action is appropriate.

Living by Your Headlights

Most of us live daily, hourly, with the assumption that we know where we're going. We might be better off not assuming so. In fact, we live by faith ... faith that there will be oxygen for the next breath ... faith that the chair or the floor will hold us up ... that the oncoming car won't swerve into our lane ... faith that our food will digest properly, our heart will go on beating, etc., etc.

E. L. Doctorow once said that writing a novel is like driving a car at night. You can see only as far as your headlights, but you can make the whole trip that way. Author Anne Lamont says of this kind of thinking, "You don't have to see where you're going, you don't have to see your destination or everything you will pass along the way. You just have to see two or three feet ahead of you. This is right up there with the best advice about writing—or life— I have ever heard."

Mind Like Water Exercises

■ *Practice Just-in-Time Living*
"You will know." Something powerful happens inside me whenever a certain friend of mine speaks those words. Up to then, my thoughts have been clogging my mental sky with traffic, circling like planes

with no permission to land, fussing over the lack of some bit of information I was convinced I needed in order to take some action. And then come those reassuring words. I am reminded, as were the prophets of old, that "it will be given you what you shall do."

In a constantly changing environment we create much difficulty for ourselves by our supposed need to know. Better to choose a just-in-time mode of operation, trusting that things will show up when we need them. Such faith points us away from the constantly shifting external world, and toward the Place from which our true strength comes. With that inner confidence, we can put our energy and attention on Now.

■ Take Necessary Precautions, Then Relax and Enjoy

These days there are many alarms, many voices telling us we can't trust, we shouldn't trust. Such fear vitiates our intelligence. Good performance is based not only on information but also on confidence, self-trust, feeling good. When I was a kid, sometimes I'd go on long car trips with my parents. Becoming drowsy as night came down, I'd snuggle down in the backseat. Lulled by the hum of the tires and bits of conversation from the front seat, I'd drift off. What a great repose that was. I was utterly safe. Everything was handled. Someone was in control.... *You will know.*

Of course, you must take the necessary steps to ensure safety and success. Buy insurance. Have regular health exams. Lock the car. But then don't fuss. Balance, always balance.

■ Stop Apologizing for Not Knowing

We harry ourselves unnecessarily by hanging on to the way we used to think and act when things were more predictable. If we come to a sudden decision or take action spontaneously we tell ourselves, "I should have known, I should have been prepared." We should stop apologizing to ourselves for doing things "just in time." Instead, have confidence to start practicing just-in-time knowing, just-in-time finding of resources, just-in-time responding to changing needs, just-in-time decision-making, just-in-time living.

What is the point of nine-tenths of the preplanning we do, anyway? It's to assure ourselves that we're safe against uncertainty. We create to-do lists in our planners and palm organizers and assure ourselves that we've scoped out the path ahead. With our goal and action plan in hand, we create a mental picture of what the successful outcome will look like. Then when change comes, we are thrown. We should ask ourselves, When does a day go as scheduled? Ever? It doesn't mean don't have goals or a plan. It means *hold them lightly,* and be audible-ready (see step 14).

■ *Redefine Interruptions*

We can lose much value when we feel interrupted, for when we feel intruded upon, we act that way. When the mind wants to stay on what we are doing, it won't give full attention to the interrupter. Acting like it's in our way, we don't really see it for what it is. The problem is when it's our spouse, or our boss, or our customer, or our kids. (Kids well know the feeling of being treated as if they're in the way.)

When we live strictly by our plan, we can miss a lot of the really good stuff of life. Being so anxious to reach our target, we act frustrated and interrupted when something looms up unexpectedly. Yet that "interruption" might be the very thing we need. It may be that we should put aside what we were so busy at, and take a side trip.

■ *Value Side Trips*

Some of the richest and most satisfying experiences in my life have been side trips. Unexpected detours. Unplanned time-outs to find out what was over the hill. I was going somewhere, and something stopped and rerouted me. I could have treated it as if it were "in my way." But I didn't. Two careers and my most significant relationship are included in this category. Think about your own most important relationships and experiences. I'm sure you'll find that some of them were side trips.

The next time you are interrupted and you feel resistance to letting the interruption have your attention, stop a moment and ask yourself, What am I afraid of? What is the worst thing that could happen here? Is this interruption possibly meant for my good? Is this another great opportunity to surrender the ego? What is the right thing to do here?

■ Do the Right Thing

In the movie *An Ideal Husband* the main character says, "So many things to do, and only one thing to be done." What is that one thing to be done? It's the RTTDMYG—the Right Thing to Do in the Moment You've Got. How do you know it from all the many other things there are to do? You do whatever it takes to bring your attention fully and one-pointedly to the Present Moment. If you are exquisitely present, the right thing will show up and it will be clear. If it isn't immediately apparent, relax and be patient. Have faith that things will be provided, as you need them. And if a side trip is in order, enjoy the ride.

With everyone around us rushing pell-mell after things, it is difficult sometimes not to hop on the treadmill with them, especially if we have become infected with a certain arrogance that assumes we are in control of everything. That way lies exhaustion and bitterness.

In all human experience there's making things happen and there's letting things happen. Being happy is a matter of doing what we can to initiate desired change, and being willing to enjoy the ride when hard paddling will get us nowhere. In attitude, we are not too lifted up in good fortune, not too cast down in ill. The Serenity Prayer says it best:

> Give me the strength to change what I can,
> the serenity to accept what I cannot change,
> and the wisdom to know the difference.

STEP 5

Balance Reason
with Feeling

To be able always to spread an aura of goodness and peace should be the motive of life.

—Paramahansa Yogananda

One of the ways to lose our balance in these times is by being oversensitive. *What did she mean by that? ... I don't have to stand for this!* Hurt feelings. Taking things personally. Pride. It takes little in a pressurized work or family situation to start such rumblings in the mind of the average person. Repeated mental replays of the triggering event build resentment until the mind is utterly distracted, emotions in chaos.

Some people hide their anger and hurt feelings under an outwardly agreeable appearance. Others react with "dirty looks" and harsh words. A third group combines coolness and violence by muttering sarcastic remarks. All types make themselves and others miserable. Resentments always carry over to others, as shown by the fact that an angry mother's milk can be harmful to her infant.

Need for Balance

If reason lacks feeling it becomes calculating, harsh, judgmental. If feeling lacks reason it becomes blind emotion. For our full functioning and enjoyment of life, reason and feeling are both needed, and must rule together. The hidden scoundrels that throw the system out of whack are our likes and dislikes.

Our cognizing intelligence registers our experience in a detached way; but then, if we allow feeling to be directed by our habituated likes and dislikes, it passes judgment on the perception in terms of pleasure or pain, sorrow or happiness. Most people assert their right to what they like and don't like, and use all their experiences merely to reinforce them. Scandalized at the suggestion that such habits are the cause of their troubles, they regard strong emotional variations as normal. Thus they're unwittingly driven by these passions—away from the happiness of their true Selves.

There is a Taoist story of an old farmer who had worked his crops for many years. One day his horse ran away. Upon hearing the news, his neighbors came to visit. "Such bad luck," they said sympathetically. "May be," the farmer replied. The next morning the horse returned, bringing with it three other wild horses. "How wonderful," the neighbors exclaimed. "May be," replied the old man. The following day, his son tried to ride one of the untamed horses, was thrown, and broke his leg. The neighbors again came to offer their sympathy on his misfortune. "May be," answered the farmer. The next week, military officials came to the village to draft young men into the army to fight a losing war. Seeing that the son's leg was broken, they passed him by. The neighbors congratulated the farmer on how well things had turned out. "May be," said the farmer.

Seeing Newly

Perhaps you've had the experience of truly being seen, as yourself, for yourself, with no assumptions. That is a rare gift that has the power to transform and affirm your ability to be your very best. Conclusion: we are not what people (including ourselves) take us for. Beyond and behind the appearance of us lies the truth of us. And real seeing—seeing freshly, without assumptions or foregone conclusions—brings forth that truth.

What if you woke up one day and found that all your assumptions were erased? A new world would open for you. You would be starting over every moment. You would see with wonder. You would look at people and events with innocence. Every experience would be fresh, an adventure into the unknown.

That's what Buddhists mean when they speak of the *beginner's mind,* and it is an aspect of Mind Like Water. Think what you could create, untrammeled by your assumptions. Your inner knowing would flourish. You would actually *see* what you were looking at, for you would bring none of your old leftover supposed "knowledge" about it to this fresh experience of it. Your seeing of it would be new. *You* would be new. The situation would never have been there for you before—*this* situation would be different from *that* situation, and it from the last.

Mind Like Water Exercises

■ *Tense and Relax*

Tense with will, directing life energy to flood the body or any body part. Then relax the tension and feel the soothing tingle of new life and vitality in the recharged area. There is a nautical phrase that was given to the helmsman regardless of sea or weather conditions, which we may well take to heart as we sail the stormy seas of life today: *Steady as she goes.*

■ *Control Your Anger*

We're all placed in trying situations from time to time, and often patience wears thin. The best defense against anger is a good offense.

Take some time at the beginning of each day to calm yourself and set the emotional stage. When you first awake, think good thoughts. Keep an inspirational book next to the bed so you can bathe the mind in positivity, even before you bathe the body in the shower.

On your way to work, purposely think positive thoughts about the day ahead. Imagine yourself proceeding calmly through even the most trying circumstances. Rather than worry about a stressful situation or interaction you anticipate, practice seeing yourself going through it without a blip on the emotional screen. Set the thermostat on that emotional temperature gauge at a cool temperature; refer to it during the day, and keep cool.

■ Identify the Signals

Learn to know the early warning signs of emotional buildup. Where do you feel anxiety—in the shoulders? neck? forehead? stomach? Know your pet peeves and the people who tend to get under your skin, the environments or situations that trigger irritation. At first warning, congratulate yourself that you have caught the signal early, and take action to wind down the stress.

■ Develop Confrontation Skills

Some conflicts are unavoidable. People are divided between *fight* and *flight* in their styles of handling interpersonal stress. Neither style is better—each has its advantages and disadvantages. If you know your style—your way of handling conflict—and affirm it, you can be relatively comfortable in an uncomfortable situation. Is your style fight, or is it flight? If it's flight, honor that. Excusing yourself from a heated discussion or a no-win situation gives time for the dust to settle, and for you and others to think more rationally.

If you are in a confrontation with someone and your style of preference is fight, use the energy and the strategic insight that are parts of your aggressive nature to get the other party into a win-win outcome. Share your feelings. This keeps blame away, keeps you congruent, and models being real to others. Examples: "I have the impression you're angry (hurt, mistrustful, resentful, etc.) with me. I'd like to hear about it"; or "When you do/say such-and-such, I feel confused (left out, threatened, disappointed, attacked, etc.)." Even better, relate your feelings to the value of the relationship, as in "I get distracted by our disagreements; they threaten our harmony and our ability to work together as a team. What would it take to work this out?"

If it's an argument or a disagreement, try to be the one who winds it down. Give up your turn and let the other go first. Use a door opener: "I'd really like to understand how you see this." Demonstrate understanding by replaying the message, focusing on the person's feelings: "So when such-and-such happened, you felt ..." or "So you didn't like it when ... because ..." Think win-win—use feelings to lead you to *needs,* and then try to find a solution that meets *all* the needs.

■ *Defuse*

One of the best ways to defuse an argument or confrontation is by creating a diversionary confusion. I call it the Columbo strategy. You remember that detective series where the star always appeared confused about something. If you look genuinely confused and ask for help, it diverts anger and allows space for the situation to cool down. At the same time, if you do it right, it focuses attention in a nonthreatening way on the issue at hand.

"I need your help in understanding this ..." or "Maybe you can explain to me..." or "There's something I don't get about this..." or even, to promote conciliation, "Maybe we're not really listening to each other here. Tell me again...." Of course, these same words can be said in a snide, sarcastic, or blaming way. Be sure you are sincerely seeking answers and not just setting up an opponent to shoot him or her down.

■ *Use the Breath*

Stress-management experts tell us that the way we breathe has a profound effect on the way we feel. One deterrent to anger is a very old one: Take ten deep breaths. If you can, make a real breathing activity of it. Sit down, close your eyes, relax, and concentrate on your breathing. Breathe slowly and deeply, then exhale and keep the breath out as long as is comfortable, all the while concentrating on the inner calmness of breathlessness.

Without controlling the breath, just observe it. Whenever the breath comes in, visualize an ocean wave spilling on a sandy beach. When it goes out, see the wave receding. Count breaths in groups of five, then five groups of five. Add a pleasant voice saying "hello" on the in-breath and "good-bye" on the out-breath.

■ Visualize

Imagine that inside of you is a castle. Draw yourself away into one of its towers. Pull up the drawbridge. Place guards at the gates. Surround the castle with an army of invincible fighters. No enemy—stress, worry, fear, or anger—can get in! Keep within your castle as you work, aware that no matter what happens, you are safe from stress, worry, fear, or anger attacks.

■ Make a Commitment

In his book *Mastery,* author and aikido teacher George Leonard extols the value of long-term, committed practice without looking for results. He writes, "'How long will it take me to master aikido?' a prospective student asks. 'How long do you expect to live?' is the only respectable response." To rewire ourselves from our accustomed state of nervous, ground-level consciousness takes a lifelong commitment. It might be years before you achieve even-mindedness, the ability to be "not too lifted up by fortune, not too cast down by sorrow." Isn't it worth it, though, not to be driven about and smashed by constantly changing conditions and circumstances?

The mantra "Perhaps I am not looking at this in its true light" is particularly useful in this Day of the Runaround. When things move fast, people get frazzled. Tempers flare as they look around for whom to blame for their discomfort or embarrassment. In these situations finding a means of working with one's own emotional states can be liberating. As we are facing a difficult event, or even right in the midst of a threatening emotional crisis, we can assist ourselves by remembering that feelings, ever and always, result from thinking. It helps to recall that our thinking creates our experience of what is real. As soon as we realize that, we are standing apart from our thinking—and already watching it change for the better.

> In relation to the knowledge of the world and of ourselves, the conditions would be ideal could we venture to accept nothing as given, and count all as demanding definition and proof.
>
> —P. D. OUSPENSKY

Balance Family
and Work

Working parents have two full-time jobs.

—Working Woman magazine

When a father of three returned home after a two-day business trip, his wife told their kids, "Say hi to your dad." "Oh, hi, Dad," they said. "Have you been gone?" In today's families, where everyone is overscheduled and rushing about, family unity may seem like a thing of the past. Busy parents worry about time not spent with their kids. Sometimes parents are also interrupted or distracted at work by home concerns. How to be effective in both environments?

For the past decade at least, with more single-parent homes and more families with two incomes, it has tended to be the home life that has suffered more than the work life. Parents can become so absorbed in their work that when they come home they feel they deserve peace and quiet. Many go through the week without much family time, promising themselves that the weekend will be the catch-up time. And that's just how it turns out—there is so much racing to catch up during that time (including shopping, house-work, yardwork, etc.) that weekends often turn out to be more hec-tic than the rest of the time. Many workers welcome the return of a predictable routine with the coming of Monday morning.

Carving out family time is no small feat for today's working parent, particularly if you are a small-business owner. The busi-ness is your biggest baby; it's on your mind almost continuously. While you're helping your daughter with her homework your mind may revolve around difficult suppliers or cranky customers.

With so many today in a 24/7 lifestyle, the phrase "Get a life" has become common advice. Many people who are suc-cessful in their work do not know how to balance their work con-cerns with their family concerns. Some become isolated behind technology; their only relationships are online. Many so-called workaholics use their business as an escape from personal rela-tionships and social commitments. Overbusy working people easily become psychologically unavailable.

If you are one of these, decide now to do something about it. Ask yourself, When I am looking back on my life, will I feel that I spent enough time with my spouse and kids? Am I sure I am really hearing what my loved ones are telling me? Do I cultivate friend-ships? During the past month, have I spent quality time with a par-ent or a sibling? Do I have to be reminded about family birthdays? How long since I've been out on a "date" with my spouse? Do I know the most pleasing or upsetting thing that has happened lately with him or her?

The Value of Spouse Time

Children aren't the only ones getting short shrift when it comes to Mom's or Dad's attention. "It's not uncommon for entrepreneurs to run through three or four spouses," says David Birch, head of a market research firm. Karlin Sloane, a clinical psychologist who runs a New York consulting group specializing in advising high-tech start-ups on workplace issues, has clients set manageable goals for their social lives.

The past few years have seen a proliferation of coaching and counseling businesses starting up. Dan Sullivan, a coach specializing in advising entrepreneurs, reports, "I believe that marriages fall apart because of the lack of free time. Not money, not sex, but time.... So we tell all of our married clients to start dating again." The advice is simple: Get a baby-sitter, get dressed up, go out to dinner or a movie, have a conversation. "If the marriage doesn't get taken care of," Sullivan concludes, "neither does the family."

Few small-business owners would disagree that the foundation of a successful business is a strong business plan. What is needed as well is a *life plan*. Most working couples are not working toward the same goals or making the same assumptions about the future—and they don't realize it. The oldest advice is the best: *Talk*. A good place to start is for both spouses to take time to rank-order the values listed below, then sit down together and compare their lists. What surprises occur? What values do they have in common? How can these values be strengthened and implemented? What values are diverse? How can each partner accommodate and support the other in fulfilling these values?

Mind Like Water Exercises

■ *Walk Your Talk*

In the end, your loved ones don't get the stuff you provide, they get *you*. Your most powerful method of influencing them is by example. Choose one of the values below and start acting it out consistently.

Calmness   Resolve to move slower, talk quieter, listen more, and be the one who stays serene when others lose their heads.

Happiness	Don't worry, be happy. Stay good to yourself. Don't let the small stuff get to you. Be a smile millionaire.
Teamwork	Start a project and invite assistance; ask for help on chores such as cooking or cleaning or washing the dog; give some responsibilities away; share the load.
Empathy	Offer a willing ear whenever it is needed; use trips to the store or sports events or music lessons to question and show understanding; make others the stars of conversations.
Relaxation	Don't bustle about all the time; set a slower pace by doing nothing on occasion; balance doing with not doing.
Exercise	Go "dream walking" around the block. Pretend you are breathing yourself forward, or that an invisible rope is pulling your down the path, or that a giant hand is at your back, pushing you along.
Just Being	Create parts of your day when your kids or spouse find you sitting with a cup of tea and a good book.

■ *Send Apprecio-grams*

Set up e-mail between family members; whenever you have a moment, send them short, instant messages of appreciation. Leave notes under pillows and in lunch boxes. Design a form resembling a telegram with blanks for writing; for example,

Dear _____ ,

I appreciate __(what person said or did)__ .

What it did for me or us was to (impact or personal benefit) .

love, _____

Photocopy the form and keep a stack handy by the bulletin board. Invite family members to complete one whenever they have something positive to say, and post it or leave it on the recipient's bed.

To start things off, deliver a sincere apprecio-gram to each family member to model the behavior and show how enjoyable it is to receive one.

■ *Institute Family Meetings*

A. Choose a purpose for the meeting. Is it to:

- Share information?
- Deepen understanding and appreciation of each family member?
- Create a family calendar for the coming month?
- Plan family activities?
- Increase positive communication?
- Solve a problem?

B. Follow guidelines:

- Each member gets a turn; he or she has the floor for up to five minutes, and is to be listened to without interruption.
- A person's turn begins by sharing something she/he appreciates.
- If a problem or complaint is brought up, it must be done respectfully and without blame. A good alternative for you to model for kids is the "I message."

  When you ___(behavior)___ , I feel ___(true feeling)___
  because ___(impact of other's behavior)___ .

- After explaining the problem, the person can then call for a two-minute family brainstorm of solutions, during which he/she writes down items. Rules of brainstorm: Anything goes. No rights, no wrongs. Record every item. Piggyback ideas. Think outside the box.
- The family then selects a solution from the brainstorm list and agrees on a plan for implementing it.

■ *Play "My Favorite Things"*

After any event the family experiences together—a meal out, a trip, or even a movie or a video watched as a group—take turns having each person share three things she or he liked about the experience.

■ *Create a Family Activity Calendar*
Do this at the start of each month, at a family meeting. Use a large sheet of paper to create a form for each week, with columns for day of month, day of week, and a separate column for each family member:

Date of Month	Weekday	Mom	Sue	Dad	Ted
30	Sunday				
31	Monday				
1	Tuesday				
2	Wednesday				
3	Thursday				
4	Friday				
5	Saturday				

Ask each family member to tell you (or enter themselves) items that are scheduled for him or her in the upcoming month—such as work items, school functions, sports and entertainment, etc.—and fill in his or her column. Post the calendar so everyone can see each person's schedule. Keep colored marking pens handy so people can add regularly to the calendar. Use stickers to denote special events.

■ *Study Family Life Together*
Watch reruns with the kids of sitcom series from the fifties or sixties such as *Leave It to Beaver, Father Knows Best,* or *The Donna Reed Show.* Talk about how family life has changed since the times these shows were made. Discuss: What things were better then? What things are better now?

■ *Do a Values Sort*
Create a list of values such as the following one, and photocopy it. After a meal or at a family meeting, give each family member a copy. Ask people to circle items that appeal to them, and to mark

their top three values. Then have them find partners and take turns sharing their choices. Each pair has five minutes to come up with three values they agree on. Next, pairs meet with pairs and negotiate the top three values. Continue until everyone in the family has agreed to the top three family values. At a future meeting, brainstorm a list of actions, rules, family policies, etc., that exemplify each of the agreed-upon values.

truth	sincerity	humor	relaxation
courage	loyalty	trust	hard work
justice	teamwork	learning	excitement
faith	friendship	love	obedience
strength	fairness	respect	fun
honor	happiness	beauty	support

(*Note:* This activity can be used at work with teams.)

■ Make a Family Bulletin Board

Put this where everyone will see it. Include notices, praisings, jokes, personal memos, special events, interest items, cartoons, awards, prizes, etc. Encourage each person to make frequent postings that keep everyone in the loop. Post pictures from work as a way to share people and events from your "other life" with family members.

■ Make Moments Count

Reframe formerly dutiful ferryings of kids to sports practices, music or dance lessons, to be special share times. Warm up these no-big-deal periods by (1) asking open-ended questions, (2) listening and showing interest without giving advice or adding your own thoughts, and (3) demonstrating understanding. Examples: "What are you excited about these days?" … "Tell me about this coach" … "What plans do you have for the weekend?" "So you liked it when …" "You're not so sure about …" "Seems you have a lot of things coming up" … "What do you think you'll do about it?" … "I think you have it handled."

■ *Esteem Yourself*

Attitude is everything. Make sure others in your family are living with a happy, fulfilled person—you. Greet yourself in the mirror each morning by using stress comedian Loretta LaRoche's pep talk: "Here I am. I'm back, and parts of me are excellent!" Practice unconditional self-esteem: appreciate your inner being and goodness, regardless of what may be going on or of what others are doing or feeling.

■ *Keep Your "I Love You's" Up-to-Date*

This useful phrase I learned from my friend Ken Blanchard. It's something we can neglect when things move fast.

Work *and* family are each more than worth the effort. By repeated prioritizing, by setting short-term goals at home and at work and sharing them with both groups, by keeping ourselves fit and healthy, by entering our day to fortify us against crippling worries and fears, and by keeping our *I love you's* up-to-date, working parents can succeed at both of their full-time jobs.

reflection

❧

Having no need to alter things or to display
or interpret them differently,
water perfectly mirrors whatever is around it.

*Lesson: Let go of your assumptions,
your preconceptions and prejudices.
Be willing to see things as they truly are.*

STEP 7

Enter Your Day

We must learn to reawaken and keep ourselves awake, not by mechanical aids, but by an infinite expectation of the dawn, which does not forsake us in the soundest sleep. I know of no more encouraging fact than the unquestionable ability of man to elevate his life by a conscious endeavor.

—Henry David Thoreau

Have you recently found yourself running so fast you need to sit down and figure out where you're going, but there's no time to do it? That's the seat of craziness. The paradox of our times is that as change accelerates, there is *greater need but less time* for us to reflect on where we are heading. Without taking time to get above the trees, we fall into the trap of doing things right but failing to do the right things. Consequently, the state of millions of busy people these days is *lost, but making great time.*

Our fast pace of life is robbing us of an inner satisfaction, the sense of rising each day to meet a promise we've made to ourselves a long time ago to fulfill our best and our highest. At times we wake with the despair that has been previously only the curse of the rich and the empty. We are rushers on the road to we're not sure where. Life rings a little hollow, and we pray, somewhere way deep inside, for a slower time, a chance to muse and contemplate and dream again.

Reflection—More Need, Less Time

As human beings we thrive on meaning. Without it, our spirits die. Goals are important, but setting and achieving short- and long-term goals is not enough. Goals are only a means to a worthwhile life. How do we know which goals are important? On any given day when all matters seem urgent, the relativity of their importance blurs. How can we keep from losing our focus? Where can we stand to gain perspective on the whole forest? How, when, or where do we get the insight to know the difference? There is only one place to start. That is with ourselves—through reflection.

Getting Found before Getting Lost

People all over the globe are hungering for a perspective that can be gained only through spiritual awakening. This awakening is available to each of us if we will learn to balance activity with reflection. Step 1, "Trust Your Intuition," is concerned with helping you begin a daily program of doing something *before* you get out in the world, where it's so easy to become spiritually lost. It shows you how to slow down before you speed up, to destress before you stress, to arm yourself with a right attitude so you won't need attitude adjustments later in the day.

All of us have had the peculiar experience of being awake while the rest of the world is asleep, when it's safe to let the heart open and the mind roam. At such moments, the silence speaks. It gives us back to ourselves with a delicious sense of aloneness sans loneliness, as when in Nature we walk on a deserted beach or in quiet forest, or sit in wonder to behold the panoply of stars flung across the night sky.

The key to the way you experience each day is the way you begin it. If you hit the ground running, you're already in trouble; you'll be running all day. Conversely, if you take time to slow down before your start—to *enter* your day—you'll already be ahead of the game. "Morning watch" is a phrase that captures that peculiar privacy, that strange sense of comforting solitude known to the early riser. The sentry standing guard is familiar with the exacting alertness with which the moments are charged, the burden of proof that rests on those shoulders to see that slumbering troops are safe. Likewise, the watcher with the sick or the dying knows the intimacy and self-reflection that attends that silent caretaking.

The goal, the thing we are watching for when we speak of a morning watch, is captured in this passage from the Bhagavad-Gita:

Steadfast a lamp burns sheltered from the wind;
Such is the likeness of the Yogi's mind
Shut from sense-storms and burning bright to Heaven.
When mind broods placid, soothed with holy wont;
When Self contemplates self, and in itself
Hath comfort; when it knows the nameless joy
Beyond all scope of sense, revealed to soul—
Only to soul!

The image of the lamp burning "steadfast" is descriptive of the state of mind that is our goal on the morning watch. Early in the day, before mundane matters begin to invade the mind, is the time to achieve an interior state comparable to the calmness of a steady candle flame. That is what we are watching for, that dawning of unruffled peace of which other hours of the day are bereft.

The morning watch is a time you set aside at the outset of each new day to nurture the realization that there is something that is far more powerful, loving, and creative than you are. The critical moment for contacting the realest part of yourself, for clarifying and aligning with your highest ideals and deepest motives, is each morning as you open your eyes. Achieving the emergence from within ourselves of that wondrous joy without which life is meaningless and drab, we can face anything the day has to throw at us. And so we wait and watch.

Mind Like Water Exercises

■ *Get Up Early*

Plan to make the first half hour you are awake a time for setting the stage for the rest of the day. Beginning tomorrow, get up at least twenty minutes earlier than has been your custom. Don't go with the protesting mind ("I don't get enough sleep as it is!" "I'm not a morning person!" etc.); instead, command the mind to start getting you to bed at least twenty minutes earlier.

A jangling or buzzing or beeping sound is not a suitable call to a peaceful wakening. Instead of subjecting your waking to such upsetting noise, plan your next waking as you are going off to sleep the night before. Determine the exact time you plan to wake up. Make your last thoughts be of waking at that earlier hour. Believe that your mental alarm will work.

■ *Control Your Opening*

The very first thoughts you think when you wake up set the stage. Your mind is like an empty room when you waken; the door to that room opens when your eyes do. Don't let the devils of stress, worry, fear, or anger get in first. If they do, they'll take over control. Don't even let yourself start thinking about the day ahead yet. There's time for that. Hold those thoughts off. Tell yourself that the first twenty minutes of each day are about setting a course.

It helps to have a cue, something on which to focus the mind while all else becomes still. This cue may be an affirmation you repeat mentally or in a whisper. Writing the cue on a card and placing it beside the bed may help. Here are some suggestions:

- I am calm, focused, and free.
- I am a time millionaire.
- I remain in the moment and go with the flow.
- My mind is saturated with peace.

Another cue is music. Some people, rather than using the mental alarm clock strategy, prefer to wake up to music. Alarm radios or CD players, set to a timer and set low in volume, can wake you to soothing or stirring strains that set the tone for your moving through the day with calmness and purpose.

Whatever cue you use, purposely make your first thoughts uplifting ones. Think about God, or a loved one, or a joyful experience. Keep an inspiring book by the bedside, and reach for it right away. Saturate your mind in positivity.

■ Go for a Dream Walk

It is advisable to make exercise a regular part of the morning routine. Some people do their workout after work, in the evening. My preference is morning, for two reasons: I'm tired later on, and it's too easy to let it go.

When you do get up, dress in loose clothes and tennis shoes, and go for a ten- to fifteen-minute brisk walk. As you walk, take your mind away from the worries and concerns of the day by inwardly chanting an affirming rhyme or phrase to walk to. (Example: *Today is before me, an untrodden dream.... I'm light as a feather, I'm not as I seem.*)

■ Inquire Within

Upon returning, sit down quietly and contemplate. Think about your values. Review your personal mission statement. (See step 19.) Write a purpose for the day. The proper order for human endeavor is: first *being,* then *doing,* then *having.* You can create a statement of your intention for the day by filling in the following three blanks:

- Today I AM _____.
  Choose the attitude which will permeate all you do today—calmness, peace, joy, focus, openness, happiness, concentration, presence of mind, friendship, etc.

- I WILL _____.
  Select three to five actions you can see yourself doing in the hours ahead that are in line with and express your chosen attitude.

- As a result, I WILL HAVE _____.
  Here note down the results—material, emotional, or spiritual—that you intend to achieve.

■ Visualize the Day Ahead

Close your eyes, relax, and visualize a day of no stress. See yourself at the end of the day looking back on a succession of hours in which your tasks seemed to do themselves through energy that flowed easily through your mind and body.

■ Pray

In whatever terms are dearest to your heart, express your reliance on Spirit. Give thanks and ask for help. Make sure that you have checked with your Inner Stage Manager before you go out onstage. In assisting with the writing and editing chores for producing the book *Everyone's a Coach,* by Ken Blanchard and Don Shula, I was particularly struck by one story we included about Shula, the winningest coach in any professional sport. Don, who had not yet retired from coaching the Miami Dolphins, was talking about the necessity of having deep convictions that would drive the leader's performance. He shared these thoughts about his habit of beginning each day:

"I try to attend Mass every day. When we're are at home, I attend a small service every morning at 6:30 A.M. Attending Mass and looking to God for guidance aren't just habits for me. They matter deeply to me when I'm out in my world of shrill whistles and clashing bodies. And when game day comes, they're ways for me to keep my perspective. It makes a real difference to me when I start off each day by giving thanks and asking for help."

■ Don't Spill the Milk

The purpose of entering your day is not merely to have a respite from daily trials; it is to set a pace for yourself which you will maintain throughout your waking hours. It is to put you in control of your mind and emotions. It is to allow you to go forward in a state of consciousness whereby, no matter what happens, you can be *calmly active, actively calm.* You don't want to lose the peace of mind your new morning routine has brought to you the minute you get out there where things are flying fast and furious. Your peace is like a pail of milk you've spent time collecting. Make sure you don't spill a drop.

Each day, follow this simple seven-step plan. You will probably see an immediate difference when you start, but don't trust that. You must not be content with a little peace. Commit to a long-term practice of peace of mind. As you seek to sail your ship through today's uncharted waters, you are at risk from storms and heavy seas. Explore the simple navigational strategy of checking your inner instruments each morning, so that by the end of that day's sailing you may yet be found on your truest course.

> Start each day by affirming peaceful, contented, and happy attitudes, and your day will tend to be pleasant and peaceful.
>
> —NORMAN VINCENT PEALE

STEP 8

Seek Silence

When you are still, you find that your perception of life is at its purest.

—RON ROTHBUN, *The Way Is Within*

The common belief that a successful person is dynamic, hard-driving, enjoys life fully, and thrives on pressure and tension leads many to associate inner tranquillity with lack of drive, inability to compete, dullness of personality. This bias against inner silence is a serious mistake. Medical professionals have long recognized that silence plays an important part in healing. For instance, the experience of even a little real silence can produce physiological changes that neutralize the effects of stress.

Dr. Hans Selye, a pioneer in the field of stress management, defined stress as "the body's nonspecific response to any demand made on it." In responding to stress, people commonly experience muscular tension, increased heart rate, accelerated breathing, sweating, and anxiety. As stress saps vitality, silence restores it; as stress lowers resistance to disease, silence raises it. In internal silence one experiences a state of deep rest. Heart rate decreases, as do oxygen consumption, perspiration, muscle tension, blood pressure, and levels of stress hormones. Beyond these physical changes, one achieves heightened mental clarity and emotional ease. Silence, then, can and should be thought of as a healer and a fortifier—a sort of conscious, controllable counterpart to the immune system.

If we were to take today's hectic lifestyle—the Runaround—as a societal pathology, we can surely agree that the "patient" needs rest and a special kind of quiet—what Harold Bloomfield, M.D., calls *internal silence*. "I can think of no more important factor in the process of healing," he writes, "than the quality of inner silence. As therapists of all types become more aware of this powerful state, great strides will be made in the science of healing."

If we are to possess and preserve an inner equilibrium to counter the craziness and noise we face in the outer world, we must practice solitude and interiorization of consciousness. This comes by achieving absolute stillness and thoughtlessness. The condition for this is silence. Silence is essential to peace of mind. Just as we need sounds and change to stimulate us each day, so we require quiet and absence of movement to maintain mental, emotional, and spiritual balance.

The Search for Silence

Silence is the condition for conducting the inner search for what we most deeply want and need. But where is this silence to be found? The world will not give you silence. You might occasionally find it—late at night, out in nature, etc.—but to achieve the silence you need every day for balancing your life, you must develop and master a technique that enables you to find it within yourself. The ability to tune in to inner silence is forged through daily practice. Left to chance, this silence will not come to you. You must create it, purposely and consciously, every day.

Mind Like Water Exercises

■ *Seek Solitude*

In this frenzied world, it is good advice to "be often alone." Without periods of interiorized reflection, the mind remains in a constant state of restlessness. While the herd is constantly driven about with the winds of change, those who quietly insist on operating from a mind like water know a secret possessed by few: aloneness protects one against the cacophony that blocks access to the really creative solutions to life's problems. The saying of Indian sages that "solitude is the price of greatness" is nowhere and at no time more true than in the West today.

■ *Listen for Silences*

When we think of listening, we think of sounds. But it is possible to listen for silences. There is so much noise, you might have to strain your ears for the moments of no noise. We can train our ears to be directional microphones, picking up selectively the sounds around us, focusing first on one, then on another. Then we can switch and listen to the spaces—the *silences between sounds*. The immediate relief that comes from only a few moments of sincere practice of this activity is surprising.

When you're listening to someone talk, focus on the spaces between his or her words. Through this practice you'll learn that none of what is said is lost; in addition, your focus causes the interaction to slow down and move toward greater truth and intimacy. As a bonus, you can entertain yourself if the person's speech is boring.

■ *Seek Your Own Counsel*

In the endless media-sponsored game of celebrities, sensationalism, fashion, and fads, everything is driven by perceptions. To have your attention constantly on "what's hot and what's not" is to be tempted away from following your own bliss. Ask not what you should want or think; ask: "What do *I* want? What do *I* think?" Get away each day, as best you can, to listen within for the still, small voice.

■ Empty the Space

Have you trained your senses to require noise? Find out by turning off your car radio or tape player. Turn off the greatest household pest, the TV. Allow yourself to be quiet around others. Listen to people without planning what to say when they take a breath. When asked a question, pause. Don't speak unless it's necessary. Spend time "alone together" with loved ones.

■ Take Silence Breaks

Some people can shut out the world at will. How do they do it? They've practiced. Sit quietly, relax, close your eyes, and lift your gaze. Spend some well-earned moments using your imagination to contact a vast inner quietude. You can use one of the following pictures, or make up your own:

> ■ Create a vast, rippleless lake lying perfectly quiet beneath a sailing moon. Watch the reflection of the moon in the water. If it's ruffled up, just relax and go deeper. Keep watching until the water becomes utterly rippleless.

Open your eyes and carry the momentary peace and calm you've earned into your duties. Keep visualizing the rippleless lake of your inner mind. Stay within your castle as you work, aware that no matter what happens, you are safe from stress, worry, fear, or anger attacks.

■ Avoid Noisy Things

Don't hang around noisy, boisterous people if you can help it. Seek instead to be with peaceful people. Even a brief phone talk with such a friend can help. Avoid noisy places filled with crowds and confusion. Instead, "take the long way home." Seek little time-outs during breaks, lunch hours, and commutes when, even for moments, you find "daisies to smell."

■ *Make Silence Your Reply When the Chips Are Down*

Silence is so powerful that it can end a heated dispute. When my brother and I were boys, we occasionally got into squabbles. Once an argument over something escalated until we were trading shouted threats and insults. I sent a particularly vitriolic message his way, then stood back, expecting to receive his verbal slap. Instead he nodded silently, turned, and walked away. The fight was over, and I was flabbergasted in soft defeat. That memory has stayed with me all my life. The following excerpt from Paramahansa Yogananda's poem "Silence" reminds us of that power:

> The tiger may be tamed,
> Failure's talons can be maimed,
> All friends forsaking reason's way regained,
> Unruly nature trained,
> By powerful silence of unspoken words,
> If in truth maintained.

■ *Learn Stillness from Nature*

Somewhere near you—it could be on "the long way home" from work—is a spot where there is a body of water, a forest, or a high point with a view. Lakes or ponds or ocean seem to give us back to ourselves when we sit for a while by them and contemplate the smooth, glassy surface or waves or ripples (perhaps we intuit kinship with the water, which undulates but does not itself move). A summit with a long vista lifts our spirits. We are quieted within by the stillness of animals, or of leaves standing still on forest trees. Let the natural elements speak to you, inducing in you more of an appetite for peace.

■ Sit in the Silence

The Psalmist sings, "Be still, and know that I am God." Within is where the stillness is, but we can't reach to it as long as the body is restless or the mind is tossing about. Sitting alert and watching the breath is a good way to find that stillness. The first thing you find is, you don't do it. So make a habit. Even two minutes of total thoughtlessness—no images, plans, memories, registering of sensations, just hearing an inner sound when the breath starts in, another when it starts out—can afford relief from the crazy world. (See step 9.)

■ Develop a Portable Quietness

The ultimate quietness is quiet on command! Accessing inner solitude is a skill we all need in turbulent times. Imagine a place in the very center of your body that is full of stillness. Go there in your mind. Stay there, letting all the urgencies go by for just a small time, then return to your duties refreshed. Or, using visualization, train yourself to visit at will a haven of quietness within yourself. I've had success bringing the image of a candle up close. I imagine its flame without a flicker, as outside I hear the noise of a gale blowing through the forest.

In the coming year, do you think you might occasionally need answers to perplexing problems and intimidating issues in your life? Of course you will. Just don't make the last place you look for them the least obvious one—within yourself. They can be found there, but only by quieting the mind and stilling the body. Get still somewhere alone, take some deep breaths, and ask a question mentally. Then go deeply inside. Be patient, watching the breath and hearing a sound with each intake and outgo, until restlessness passes. Let the mud settle to the bottom, and there, unseen before, you will find your solution.

STEP 9

Learn to Meditate

The joyous rays of the soul may be perceived if you interiorize your attention. These perceptions may be had by training your mind to enjoy the beautiful scenery of thoughts in the invisible, intangible kingdom within you.

—PARAMAHANSA YOGANANDA

They say that if you repeat an action that you perceive as having personal value for twenty-one consecutive days, you are likely to become what writer William Glasser calls "positively addicted" to the practice. That is, you will have received enough benefit that you will miss doing it if you stop. That was my experience with meditation. I had spent several years sporadically "sitting in the silence" without the knowledge or the benefit of any specific techniques. Finally I signed up for the yoga meditation lessons from Self-Realization Fellowship, the Los Angeles–based organization founded by Paramahansa Yogananda. Receiving the weekly SRF lessons—clear instructions on how to meditate that include practical guidelines for living a spiritual life in a busy world—I began immediately to practice the techniques.

One evening after only a few weeks of my own practice, I was finishing my fifteen-minute meditation. I had evidently reached a level of consciousness beyond the usual, and was returning to the world from which I'd been away, when in a sudden flash of illumination I glimpsed the illusory nature of that material world. In a split second, the universe I'd been accustomed to think of as real was revealed to be a dream. This was not an intellectual conclusion; I could not have deduced it. It was a moment of truth, intuitively perceived.

Carl Jung's study of the practice of yoga led him to declare that it offered "undreamed-of possibilities." That single moment of truth blessed me with its illumination. It acted as a "divine come-on" to keep me learning and practicing, and from that day twenty-two years ago I have never looked back. I continue to consider meditation far and away the most important thing I do.

Why Meditation?

Mind Like Water is so different from the way we have accustomed our minds to think that it requires its own training ground. The busy world is no place for this training—the busy world is what we need to escape! We are trying to develop calmness and aboveness, but how do we do it? By three basic steps:

- Seeking solitude
- Turning attention away from the outer world, and within
- Concentrating away from thoughts stimulated by external focus

The most fundamental and long-proved method that incorporates these essential steps is meditation.

Why has meditation stood the test of time? Why have people of various ages and cultures found their way to this same practice? It is because meditation is really the only way to get out of our movie—to temporarily escape the dreamlike drama in which we tend to see ourselves trapped. (Most people would not think of themselves as "trapped" in a certain version of reality, but many think of themselves as trapped in their bodies, or in their jobs, or in their relationships, or in their chaotic lifestyles. It's the same thing—we are what we think.)

Meditation alone offers an alternative to defining existence solely on the basis of information brought to us by our senses and by our process of rational inference based on those sensory data. Does meditation sound like a panacea? Find out for yourself! By no other method of self-effort can you deliberately and consciously produce your own peace of mind. And when you have that, everything in your experience changes.

As in the example of the fish that is told it is in water and replies, "Water? What water?" our definition of reality is so "there" for us that we do not see it. We cannot imagine anything else being real. Furthermore, we don't realize that we are producing and maintaining that view of things ourselves, often at considerable psychic cost. Our material reality hides the spiritual Reality behind everything, behind the way we see ourselves. So accustomed are we to being *in* the world that we do not know that we are not *of* the world. We are not by nature restless, driven, fearful beings hounded by implacable space-time forces. Meditation allows us to rediscover the truth of our souls—that underneath all that movie-based stuff we are pure, calm, and blissfully happy.

Isn't it amazing that on the surface we can be restless and harried, while beneath that activity the soul—the real Self—is happy? How can we dig down to that buried treasure? By using the pickax of meditation. Freed temporarily from the continual stress and hurry of restless thoughts and actions, the meditator seeks the reality of his true Self—and to his or her limitless satisfaction, finds it.

Congenial Effects of Meditation

Many are the life-enriching benefits of the practice of meditation. They could never be listed in full. Here I point out only a few salient outcomes.

Super-Consciousness

Some people think of meditation as a sort of trancelike state, a daze, or even a state of unconsciousness. Nothing could be more mistaken. When you truly meditate (and this might occur just for occasional moments during your early practice) you are outside thought, outside feeling, wonderfully calm, alert, and objective. You are more conscious than ever, for you are not at all at the effect of conditions and circumstances with which you wrestle during all those other, hurried waking hours of your life. Until you meditate, you are not conscious of how harried and laden you were. Now, suddenly freed of these burdens, you experience the first real relief you have known since the last meditation. Looking back from that height, waking consciousness is seen to be sleepwalking.

Sometimes there comes a specific letting-go moment when the mental chain connecting you with the worrisome world snaps apart, and the mind floats free, weightless. Your spirit relishes the change. *Ah, this is what I was needing!* You have come away from the world for a time, away to your own truth. Peace is the first salutary effect. As you go deeper, wisdom and great joy emerge. You are engaging with the soul, feeling, *This is where my life really is. This is really me.*

Health and Wholeness

Carl Jung, after studying the effects of yoga meditation on subjects, declared that the practice holds "undreamed-of possibilities." Realizing its health-giving benefits, many medical researchers today recommend meditation for their patients. Bernie Siegel, M.D., whose studies of healings of cancer patients through nontraditional means such as meditation, visualization, and prayer are finding increasing acceptance among allopathic physicians, says of meditation, "I know of no other single activity that by itself can produce such a great improvement in the quality of life."

In recent decades brain-wave studies have demonstrated the calming effects of meditation, as well as its ability to heighten awareness and provide control over stress. Deep meditation is characterized by high alpha/theta activity in the brain. Studies of the great increase of alpha in the right temporal lobe (the so-called right brain) have shown that depressed, introverted people have more alpha in the left fronto-temporal region (left brain), while optimistic, extroverted people have more alpha in the right side. According to research, an increase of alpha in the right brain counteracts stress and depression. The considerable increase in alpha and theta activity in most regions of the brain after meditation indicates that the brain is deeply relaxed and focused following the session.

These effects should not be surprising if you consider that meditation is soul restoration. When by the practice of meditation you find yourself outside the dream of material existence, you rediscover the basic goodness that has lived within you all along.

Freedom from Fear

The uncertainties caused by rapid change have ushered in a pervasive low-grade anxiety that places people under constant inner stress. Many wake each morning to an undifferentiated feeling of dread, and go through the routines of the day with a gnawing uncertainty about their ability to cope with the future. It's all too easy to feel victimized by the waking world. In this era the velocity of unending change can become a taskmaster, a fearsome enemy that steals the joy and serenity from life and replaces them with fear, anxiety, and restlessness. A mind that has aligned its pace to the rat race does not know how to be still; it constantly squirms and fidgets.

The closest we can come today to having an inner castle that fortifies us against all the outward foes that would bother our days and steal our peace is through the practice of solitude and inner silence. The raging storms of doubt, stress, and indecision are quieted when we learn to interiorize the mind. The masters teach that when we meditate deeply and practice the presence of the divine, we discover unlimited resources that can restore our confidence and deepen our faith.

Creative Solutions

Fill a jar with water from a raging muddy river, and set it aside for a time. When you return, the silt has settled to the bottom, and the water is crystal clear. That is an apt metaphor for the active influence of meditation on the mind. By going within and becoming calm we let the mental silt in the muddy water from the churning river of change settle to the bottom; then we can see clearly the path to take. There was the answer all the time, obscured by the gales and floods of the rushing mind.

Release of one's innate creativity is a definite outcome of steady meditation. Unique solutions and novel ideas emerge when the mind is utterly calm and receptive. Since meditation bypasses rational thought, it trains us to contact our inner knowing, intuition, that sees solutions to problems that lie outside the normal field of intellectual functioning.

> It is not a pumping in from the outside that gives wisdom; It is the power and extent of your inner receptivity that determines how much you can attain of true knowledge, and how rapidly. You can quicken your evolution by awakening and increasing the receptive power of your brain cells.
>
> —PARAMAHANSA YOGANANDA

Spiritual Transcendence

In India a parable is told likening a person to a donkey carrying sacks of gold on its back, that never looks up from plodding on its weary way to realize and appreciate the treasure that is available. Through the practice of meditation we realize that all along there was something tremendous within us, and we did not know it.

Paramahansa Yogananda, the great spiritual teacher of meditation, wrote: "Your being has two sides—one visible, the other invisible. With open eyes you behold objective creation, and yourself in it. With closed eyes you see nothing, a dark void; yet your consciousness, even when dissociated from form, is still keenly aware and operative. If in deep meditation you penetrate the darkness behind closed eyes, you behold the Light from which all creation emerges. By deeper *samadhi,* your experience transcends even the manifested Light and enters the All-Blissful Consciousness— beyond all form, yet infinitely more real, tangible, and joyous than any sensory or supersensory perception."

How to Meditate

There are many schools and techniques of meditation. My attempt here is to present some simple guidelines so the reader can get started. Once on your way, you can seek books or teachers to take you further. The key elements I will treat are posture, breathing, and concentration.

Posture

All brands of meditation stress the importance of sitting posture. The reason for this is that proper meditation induces the flow of subtle currents of energy through a series of energy centers in the spine. When these centers open up as a result of meditation practice, the meditator experiences first great peace, then deep wisdom, and finally joy or bliss. Primarily, the posture calls for the spine to be erect and firm, yet at the same time relaxed. Here is where the seating support plays a part. Sit forward on an armless chair, on which you have arranged a pillow or a combination of pillows so that the back part of your support is higher and slants your body forward:

This will support the spine and prevent slumping or straining to hold yourself up. Feet should be flat on the floor, chest out, shoulders down and relaxed, hands resting in the lap, palms upward. The head should be held with the chin parallel to the floor.

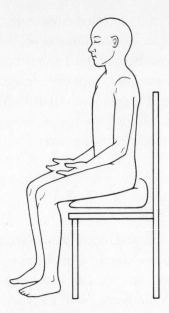

(You can imagine there is a string coming out of the center of the top of your head, from which your body is dangling.) The eyes are closed, with the gaze lifted to the point between the eyebrows (to keep the mind alert and prevent drowsiness).

Breathing

Take a long, deep breath, holding the air in the lungs for several seconds, then exhale. Repeat this eight to ten times, gradually lengthening the breath. As you do so, be aware of drawing the breath downward by the action of the diaphragm. Rather than puffing out the chest, purposely distend the lower abdomen to "belly-breathe." Think of the breath falling in, and rising out, in response to the action of the diaphragm. After these first deep, long breaths, breathe normally, still breathing from the belly.

Concentration

Often meditation teachers speak of "throwing the mind a bone." This means to provide an object for the mind to fasten its attention on and busy itself with. Such a point of concentration helps to draw the mind away from thoughts. Thinking (imagining, remembering, planning, fantasizing, processing sensations, analyzing, worrying, visualizing, etc.) and meditation are mutually exclusive. This does not mean that thoughts are bad or that they will stop; it means that we are concerned here with something different from thoughts. In meditating, the spotlight of attention is drawn out of the "thought stream" on which it is focused at most other times.

Put all your attention on a process that goes on naturally and normally all the time, although usually beneath your awareness: your breathing. With your focus at the nostrils, observe the breath closely. Note precisely when each breath starts to come in and when it starts to go out. Do not try to measure or control the breath in any way. Merely stand aside from it and watch it. Let it be all right if the breath is long or short, rhythmical or not, or if it stops either at the end of inhalation or an exhalation, or midway through one or the other. Take each breath as it comes, just as if you are observing another person's actions.

After watching the breath for a couple of minutes, add a pair of separate mental sounds, one for the inbreath, one for the outbreath. You will chant these sounds mentally, "hearing" them inwardly, in association with the breath. Rather than preceding or coinciding with the breath starting in or out, let the sounds *follow* the breath slightly.

What sounds should you use? That is entirely up to you. Rather than prescribing the sounds, here are guidelines for choosing them. First, they should be meaningless syllables rather than known words. (Think, e.g., of the musical scale: *do, re, mi, fa, so, la, ti, do.* You could select one of these items for the sound associated with inhaling, and another for exhaling.)

You could simply make up two syllables that work for you. In any case, be sure that the sounds you select are single syllables, that they seem to work together harmoniously with the inhaling and exhaling in a certain flow. If necessary, experiment until you find the right combination. Best of all is to let the sounds, by a process of intuition, "choose you." Use these same sounds each time you meditate, so they become an integral part of your technique of concentration.

An important rule, particularly for beginners, is not to look for any results from meditation. You are not trying to get anywhere, or to produce any certain experience or effect. Put yourself in the role of an experimenter: you are doing this to see what will happen, and to see how good you can get to be at it. I have heard people say that the first thing you learn when you start to meditate is that you can't do it. They are referring to the habit of the mind to go wandering off from the breath and mantra (the sounds) and into thinking again. This will definitely happen (it happens for people who have been meditating for years), but don't be concerned. Never punish yourself for your inability to concentrate. Merely notice that you are thinking (one teacher says, hear the word "thinking!" to wake yourself up to the process), and bring your mind back to the breaths and sounds.

The Western mind, accustomed to defining success by activity and achievement, is not predisposed to "sitting and doing nothing" and may see it as a waste of time. One of the hardest things for busy people is to interiorize, to shift the focus of their attention from outward-bound (communicating with the world through the senses) to inward-bound (communicating with the soul). You may encounter mental resistance in the form of beliefs and attitudes. When you sit to meditate, your restless mind may start thinking of one thing after another that you should be doing instead of this. Fidgeting, itching, aches, or tics may come; let them pass. Pay no attention.

So habituated are most people to external focus, it is extremely difficult for them to sit still for even a few minutes. The mind, surging with thoughts of all the things that suddenly need doing, puts up a fight. Thus the person must begin a training of the mind that has been compared to the training of an unruly dog; the adept is able to bring his or her mind to "heel" on command.

The goal of this training is to disregard thoughts. Meditation cannot proceed as long as the mental "space" is occupied by memories, plans, sensations, visualizations, and endlessly turning thoughts. In India, where spider monkeys are commonly seen leaping ceaselessly between the branches of trees, they have for centuries spoken of the "monkey mind." The first thing you are likely to discover about meditation is that you are not doing it! Each time the mind is drawn away into thoughts, as soon as you notice that it has done so, say inwardly the word "thinking!" and return the attention gently but firmly to the breaths and sounds.

But when do we get to the actual meditating part? Beginners will find that concentrating the mind and bringing it back from thoughts, as described above, is more or less a full-time job. After this is mastered, the person will naturally and intuitively be led to a source of actual esoteric meditation techniques. There are many teachers, classes, and books on meditation. (For those who are serious about becoming meditators, I strongly recommend that you contact the headquarters of Self-Realization Fellowship, at 3880 San Rafael Avenue, Los Angeles, CA 90065. You can receive, practically free of charge, an entire set of lessons sent in the mail, giving practical step-by-step instructions developed by Yogananda to fit the Western mind.)

Mind Like Water Exercises

■ *Use a Cue*
During long periods of work, stop a moment and isolate attention on an "item"—an image, phrase, song, or symbol—that can remind you to focus on the positive. Each time your thoughts wander ahead, to the responsibilities of the day—meetings, projects, deadlines, etc.—bring them back to the item.

■ *Solve a Problem*

You can devote occasional sittings to contemplation of a problem. Before starting, ask for guidance. Through practice of concentration you can learn to withdraw thought and energy from outward distractions and focus them on any goal to be achieved or problem to be solved.

■ *Observe the Thought Stream*

You can easily discover how your thought stream works by sitting for two or three minutes, closing your eyes, and watching carefully for the next thought. By doing so, you can determine how one thought leads to another, without any planning or choosing on your part. (This is one of the best ways to discover the truth of the statement that we do not choose our thoughts, they choose us.)

■ *Visualize*

Meditation brings the calmness in which we can see how to think clearly about something and what if any action to take. Sit and observe the breaths. Visualize a "stress thermometer" with a high reading. Breathe deeply and watch as the temperature reading lowers.

■ *Bring to Mind*

Pause now and put your attention on your heart. Feel its steady, reliable beating. Think how it does its work faithfully, day in day out, one beat at a time, without your conscious awareness. Think how the blood rushes out, replenishing the cells of nerves, bones, and muscles so you can function effectively in the world. Now observe your breathing and realize that this life-giving process, as well, proceeds most of the time beneath your awareness. Imagine the work of digestion and assimilation this moment within your body. Realize that your brain and nervous system are—again, without your help—enabling you to read these words, think these thoughts, and imagine these processes. Finally, recall that millions of disease germs are potentially around you and within your body, but that they are rendered harmless by the body's immune system, always on the alert to protect you and shield you from harmful injury or sickness. Appreciate the fact that they are going on independently of your thought, allowing you moment by moment to exist and function in the world as a contributing being.

■ *Tune In*

Pause briefly during your hours of work today and think about the power of one of your body's involuntary systems—say, the immune system. Tune in to its great reserve of power, realizing that the work of protection against disease is being carried out below your conscious awareness—merely by your being physically alive. Realize that just as that system is ongoing—on its own, as it were—your thoughts and actions also proceed more or less independently. You do not choose your thoughts, they merely pass through your mind and out again. When you want to respond to a thought or a motivation by physical action, you do not have to "take thought" about how to move your arms or hands or eyes, or how to process information that comes to you, as through this reading. That, also, proceeds without you, through the efficiency of habit. Appreciate this!

By meditation practice you begin to tune yourself in to true reality. You begin to see things—including yourself—as they are, without blame or harshness, without self-deception or excuses. You align yourself with the uncontrived order that exists in the world. You celebrate, seeing life—regardless of what else is going on—as a very special occasion.

absorption

꧁

No matter what object is thrown into a body of water, it responds appropriately. It does not get ready, it does not flinch or react. It merely receives, and returns once again to a placid state.

Lesson: Regardless of what comes your way, take it calmly and gratefully, never personally.

STEP 10

Take Stock

The greatest discovery in our generation is that human beings, by changing the inner attitudes of their minds, can change the outer aspects of their lives.

—WILLIAM BLAKE

In the midst of writing this book, I had a strange dream, induced no doubt by all the thinking and writing I was doing about the increase in the velocity of change and its effects on people. I still think it provides a pretty fair view of how things look and feel in our world today.

In my dream I watch as a gigantic man sits staring at a mammoth television set. On its screen the events of the present world are playing out. Everything that is happening on earth is miraculously unfolding simultaneously on that screen. From time to time the giant roars with laughter; at other times his bushy brow puckers in a frown. I marvel at this explanation of reality: the universe is nothing but a vast movie, playing solely for the entertainment of a stupid ogre.

As I watch, the giant reaches forward and pushes the fast-forward button on his VCR. Instantly the images on the screen begin to move faster. Pleased with this result, the grinning colossus starts punching the button again and again, delighting with each acceleration of the world scene. Watching this is upsetting; I pity the suffering I see in the anxious faces of the people on the screen. They can feel their world moving faster, like a gigantic treadmill gone berserk, but they cannot understand why this is happening. All they can do is run faster, trying to stay on top of the chaos. At this point I awake.

I think of this dream when I look at the faces of people I see as I walk down a street, enter places of business, or drive my car in traffic. These citizens of the land of Runaround could be the actors portrayed on the dream giant's dream television. They complain that they have too much on their plate, too many balls in the air, too little time. They're always behind, never caught up. They keep planners, consult Palm Pilots, make to-do lists, check beepers, e-mails, voice-mails, and work feverishly to clear their inbaskets and tickler files. Each day they hit the ground running, maintain a killing pace, and catch a few hours of fitful sleep, only to start the rat race all over again. Having lost control of things, constantly in a whirlwind of existence, they are plainly getting the Runaround.

The rushing kind of response appears to be the only choice open to ambitious, action-oriented people as they pursue success—as well as to average citizens just trying to make a living. In the clamor to grasp that ever-eluding brass ring, few stop to consider the long-term deficits of this style of pursuit. Some are physiological—the body and the nerves suffer from such unrelenting stress. The worst impact is on the psyche. The *what's-next* syndrome, for large numbers people, has become addictive.

It took you a long time to get into this rushing lifestyle, and there are many supports around you each day for continuing it (not the least of which are the actions of people around you). To begin developing a less hectic lifestyle, the old rule of "the best defense is a good offense" applies. It's time for you to take charge of your own speed. It's time to slow down and listen to yourself, to question what you are really after.

The writer David Whyte is a great advocate of setting things up for stumbling upon the truth of our lives. His words, as he applies a theme from Dante's *Commedia* to help his clients and readers to reframe their career journeys, cut deep:

> To find the real path, we have to go *off* the path we are on now, even for an instant, and earn the privilege of losing our way.... Becoming aware of this after a lifetime of accepting success as the ultimate healing balm, as something that will give you protection, is, declares Dante, like waking in a dark wood. He begins by admitting that the human mind never sees success as "here," but always ahead, down the road. He says that the day when you have your desk finally cleared will not arrive. That the level of safety you are aiming for on the corporate ladder is an illusion. He says the child you have at home, for whom you are making many sacrifices, will be grown and gone by the time you struggle back through the traffic. He says you must look hard at the road you are taking now as much as the hoped-for destination. You must admit what you see on that road and grieve long for what you do not. Then you have a possibility of waking.

Mind Like Water Exercises

■ *Find Out if You're Hooked on Speed*

A simple operative definition of addiction is that doing without the thing you're hooked on brings discomfort. To tell if you're addicted to speed (not the drug, the Runaround), stop right in the midst of a busy day, sit down, and try to calm your mind. If, despite your best efforts, your thoughts keep racing even after two minutes, chances are you're hooked.

What does it mean to be hooked on speed? It means that from the moment you wake up until you lie down at night, your thoughts are rushing pell-mell, and your actions echo your thoughts. So accustomed have you become to this feverish pace that you feel you have no choice about the sheer volume of tasks and responsibilities you face each day. You have little or no discretionary time. You do your weekends and even vacations at the same furious pace. You can't imagine how it is to live otherwise, for you don't feel in control. But given the choice to slow down, you won't do it. Boredom sets in. You must be off—immediately, hell-bent to somewhere. As soon as you're busy again, you feel relief.

■ Go Inside

Recovering from any addiction can be painful. It requires extreme self-control to persist through the discomforts, to disobey the screaming inner voices. The first and most powerful step you can take to escape Runaround is *interiorizing*—shifting your focus from your environment to your "invironment"—the perceiving mind itself. This means that while you are in action, doing whatever you do in your busy days, you practice standing aside momentarily and monitoring what is going on, inside and out. *What am I doing? Does it make sense to me? What am I feeling? Am I at peace and content? Is my mind on what I am doing, or is it up ahead, straining to get to the next thing?* Just observe, without having to do anything about what you see.

■ Get Over Yourself

Perhaps you're one of those people who think that if you stopped for even a moment from running about, keeping all those plates twirling on sticks, things in your world would go to pot. If so, recall what happens when you are ill. Somehow, the world goes on without you. Sick days are a way of finding out that your busy lifestyle doesn't need you; you need it. If you're serious about seeking an alternative to the blurring pace of your life, begin right now to take independent action. Realize humbly that you are dispensable, and act like it.

■ *Place Value on Changing Your Mind*

You may not be able to control or change the world, but you *can* regain control over your mind. It's your mind, not the world that has run away like an unruly dog. Your task is to bring your mind back and make it heel. When you do, you'll see that it's not the world that needs changing, but the way you look at the world. By changing your own mind, you are working where you can do some good. Plus, you are doing your part to make a crazy world less crazy.

Changing your mind is something you've done many times successfully in the past. Recall a job, person, place, or situation you changed your mind about. (Typical is a bad first impression on meeting someone, which becomes modified in time as you get to know the person.) Appreciate the fact that you can now bring this natural, unconscious process to cognition and *deliberately* shift your opinion or point of view about something.

■ *Zoom Out*

Human beings have the wonderful capacity to both think and be aware that they are thinking. Bump a part of your consciousness out to a point slightly above your body and to the left and rear, looking down on yourself. From this ceiling-level vantage point you can see into your mind. Train yourself to "zoom out" whenever you feel the first signs of stress or anxiety. Discover by observation what those first signs are. Develop an early-warning system that can slow you down *before* you start to speed up.

■ *Decide What's Important*

Everything these days, it seems, is urgent. But is it important? And how do you know if it's important? Begin to look at your to-do lists in a new way, by calming the clamoring voice that seems to go with each and every task, and measuring that item against an inner ruler of importance. *Which things mean the most? How will I feel if I don't complete this task? Will I sleep better tonight if I do*

this one? Which actions will bring me contentment by fulfilling my
values?

The times we live in are ideal for conducting a thoroughgoing re-examination of the way we think. The pain of failure from using outworn methods is forcing us to reexamine our long-held assumptions. Exclusive use of the old rational-logical mode has resulted, to use an old expression, in our having painted ourselves into a corner. There is no way out but up; we must transcend the mind that figures things out and begin to trust in, and glide with, the mind that knows already.

F. Scott Fitzgerald said that the measure of a person's intelligence is his or her ability to hold two apparently conflicting ideas in the mind at the same time. That is what we must be willing to do—hold an old belief lightly, while considering an alternative that may work better. Mind Like Water, it turns out, is that alternative.

STEP 11

Manage Attention

Happy the man, of mortals happiest he,
Whose quiet mind from vain desires is free;
Whom neither hopes deceive, nor fears torment,
But lives at peace, within himself content.

—GEORGE GRANVILLE

Sometimes we gain more if we are able to give up our stubborn thought limitations. The following moral/ethical dilemma was once actually used by a major company as part of a job application:

You are driving along on a wild, stormy night. You pass by a bus stop, and you see three people waiting for the bus:

1. An old lady who is about to die
2. An old friend who once saved your life
3. The perfect man/woman you have been dreaming about

Knowing that there could only be one passenger in your car, which one would you choose? You could pick up the old lady and save a life. Taking the old friend who once saved your life would be the perfect chance to pay him back. But in either case, you may never be able to find your perfect dream lover again.

The candidate (who was hired out of two hundred applicants) answered: "I would give the car keys to my old friend, and let him take the lady to the hospital. I would stay behind and wait for the bus with the woman of my dreams."

The secret of successful living is attention management. At any given moment your life of experience is directed by whatever is on your mind—what you are noticing. Many of the items you pay attention to influence your moods and emotions; you cannot regard them without feeling something about them. Attention, the mind's "noticing tool," acts like a searchlight; it lights up whatever it is pointed at, and leaves the rest dark. That's why the skill of managing your attention is so vital.

Most people do not think about their attention; they couldn't say at any certain moment what they're attending to. Consequently they give a great deal of energy to things they shouldn't. They get off track easily. They are influenced by other people and media to think in certain ways, believe certain things, like and dislike the same ideas, and as a result disregard their own counsel. In this age of information overload, the average person's mind is in a state of constant distraction. It jumps about continuously, often randomly. As soon as it attempts to pinpoint its focus, the searchlight has shifted.

When Thoreau said that the richest person is he who can afford to leave many things alone, he was speaking of the contents of consciousness. The old joke about the problem of walking and chewing gum at the same time has truth in it. Boiled down to its essence, attention management consists of focusing where we choose to be attending to, one thing at a time, by an act of will. The term "multitasking" has become common in computer circles, and people are starting to apply it to themselves. Strictly speaking, there's no such thing. We're not wired to multitask. Your attention may switch back and forth between two objects with lightning speed, but it is still doing what it is designed to do: attend to one thing at a time.

Attention is energy. In making our minds try to do more than one thing at a time we create stress and invite mental exhaustion.

As workplaces speed up and lean down, employees are asked to do more with less—and faster. Consequently many workers these days resemble circus performers; they are like jugglers balancing balls on sticks with their chins while keeping a steadily growing number of fiery rings in the air. They are teetering tightrope walkers trying to keep their balance by splitting their time and energy between projects. The commonly heard sayings "too much on my plate" and "too many balls in the air" express the burdens people are normally feeling in business and home life. The resulting distractions lead to wasted time, duplication of effort, missed opportunities, errors in judgment, false assumptions, and bad decisions.

Mind Like Water Exercises

■ *Track Your Attention*

The question "Where is your attention now?" is the basis of an enlightening (and possibly even transforming) experiment you can do right now. Take a piece of paper and a pencil and for two minutes list the objects of your attention. Write down a word or phrase designating each new object to which the beam of your attention shifts. (Examples: *birdsong ... itch ... childhood memory ... traffic sounds ... white wall ... breathing,* etc.)

Now that you've done the exercise, you are doubtless convinced that your mind, when undirected, does indeed jump about on its own fairly continuously. You also might notice a subtle sharpening of attention, a calmer attitude than before you did the experiment. If so, you might deduce that when the mind is focused on only one thing at a time, it is more alive, more relaxed and focused. If even that small practice of "attention-tracking" produces these effects, consider the awesome, laserlike mental power you could bring to bear on any issue or problem if your attention were normally under your conscious control!

■ *Develop a Laser Mind*

Concentration, as defined by the sage Paramahansa Yogananda, is "that power which one can apply negatively to free the attention from objects of distraction, and positively to place the attention on a single idea or object at a time." All truly effective people have trained themselves to concentrate, to direct their thoughts or efforts. The fact that their minds are not bothered by distractions gives to the searchlight of their attention the power of a laser beam.

The light analogy is an apt one. The undisciplined mind is like a lightbulb; it diffuses light in every direction. Its attention is low-grade with regard to any one of its objects, as it is spread all over the place. The laser-beam mind, on the other hand, is one-pointed. Gathering all its energy into one direction, it can burn quickly and efficiently through a problem.

In an information age, management of the attention searchlight is crucial for success in any endeavor. There's so much out there, there's no hope of responding to it all. You must decide ahead of time what your values are and what business you're in, then manage your attention to focus on those things and ignore all the rest.

■ *Withdraw Attention at Will*

The ancient Indian seer Patanjali first established the foundations of the science of yoga. The purpose of this science, he wrote, is "to neutralize the transformations of the thinking principle." These transformations are the things that distract us—noises, movements, odors, pains and other sensations, restless desires, fluctuations of emotions, moods, random thoughts, memories, etc. The person of concentration has learned to do away with distractions by consciously withdrawing attention from them. A scientific technique of freeing one's attention from the objects of distraction (both inner and outer) is the only way to get results.

This may sound simple, but it's useful to break it down. There are two aspects to developing concentration. The first is the ability to withdraw attention completely from distracting elements. The second is to place it on the object of choice and keep it there. The negative side of the technique involves two steps: acknowledging the distracting item your attention is aimed at, and consciously removing it. The positive aspect also consists of two separate functions: placing your freed attention on your intended object, and keeping it there until you choose to remove it.

■ Practice Switching Attention

Take two objects (say, a pen and a paper clip) and set them before you, about twelve inches apart. Put all your attention on one object. Think of aiming a spotlight at it. For half a minute or so, notice everything you can about it. Prepare to consciously remove your attention and place it on the other object. Remove it, and place it fully on the other object. Keep it there, unwavering, for half a minute, noticing the details, continuing to discover new things about it. Then remove the beam of your attention from that second object and place it back on the first. By doing this apparently simple task several times with full concentration, you may have noticed some things:

- You were distracted at some points.
- You found your mind wandering—questioning, remembering, feeling sensations, or wanting to jump off the object on which you'd fixed your attention.
- It's not that easy!

Doing such a simple activity, you might have felt patronized, but the kindergarten aspect of it is well advised. If your legs are injured and you have to learn to walk again, you will take baby steps at first. The purpose of having you do "baby steps" with attention-switching is to heighten your awareness of what it means to pay attention. It is a little like what your mechanic is up to when he or she idles the engine of your car and listens closely to it. Where are the problems and possible glitches when you purposely switch your attention at will, or keep it focused at will?

■ *Make Your Mind* Mind!

If you're like me, your mind doesn't want to be controlled. Like an unruly dog, it doesn't respond well to the leash, much less to the command "Heel!" Right now, just from where you sit or stand, mentally answer the following questions, pausing to consider each one if you need to do so. Ask yourself:

- Where is my attention right now?
- Can I name the precise object of my attention?
- Once I know where it is, do I keep it there?
- If not, does my attention leave its target unbidden, or do I choose to switch it?
- If it moves away, can I bring it back?

A few minutes of this discipline every so often each day, in the normal course of activities, will begin to get your "attention muscles" in shape. Be patient. If you're like me, the first thing you'll notice about the practice of attention management is how infrequently you do it.

Don't be surprised if the mind doesn't want to obey. It took a long time for your mind to develop its habit of distractibility. Rather than expect to turn that habit around in a day, commit to long-term practice. After all, it was only through lots of practice—albeit unconscious practice—that you managed to train the mind to its present lack of focus.

■ *Find Your Attention*

Every so often, check in with your mind by asking yourself, "Where is my attention now? And now? And now? This is a short form of the attention-tracking exercise you did on paper; it can have the same focusing effect.

■ *Know Your Chief Distractors*

Try to identify, just by observing, your own particular chief distractors, or CDs. Are they coming from inside (worries, frets, fears, unpleasant memories)? Or from outside (sounds, movements, particular environments or people)?

■ Come Unstuck

Note each time these CDs hook your attention away. Practice using the three-step method: (a) calmly, without any self-blame, notice that your attention is on the CD; (b) consciously remove it (visualize picking up your attention from the surface of the object); then (c) place it back where you want it.

■ Check Direction

During work, at times become conscious of what the goal or objective is of whatever you're doing. Occasionally move your attention away from the task, momentarily light up the target, then bring the focus back to what you're doing.

■ Focus on the Breath

Once in a while as you are working, switch your attention searchlight to your breathing. Without controlling, notice when each breath goes out. Occasionally place your attention on your heart, thinking, "You there, faithfully doing your work. You never do more than one thing at a time. Let me act more like you."

Attention is all there is. One's life consists solely of what one pays attention to. Amid turbulent days the mind is lured this way and that; attention becomes scattered, unfocused, blurred. Work, health, and relationships suffer. The ability to manage our own attention is crucial to our success and happiness. We can cure our minds of restlessness by taking charge of our attention—knowing where it is at all times, and being able to shift it or maintain it indefinitely at will.

STEP 12

Work Unattached

Even as the ignorant perform actions with attachment and hope of reward, so the wise should act with dispassionate nonattachment, to serve gladly as a guide for the multitudes.

—PARAMAHANSA YOGANANDA

Regardless of our job or profession, all of us today live and work in a service economy. You are in the service business. You have customers. This Mind Like Water step about working unattached is presented in the context of work as service. It can be applied to any area of work, because the secret of nonattachment is not in the nature of our work but how we perform it. It is not in setting our destinations but in how we make the journey to them.

These are tough, demanding times to be in business. Virtually every organization is at risk in a way it was not before, for in a global economy competitors are worldwide. Constant change and increasing complexity rule the workplace. In ever-increasing ways, workers are being asked to partner in their employer's push toward success, to push the limits of their discretionary time, effort, and thinking, to contribute more. Competition is hot. Companies and small businesses die every day, for high standards of quality of product and excellence of service are now only requirements for getting on the playing field. Customers are picky. Owners are demanding. Bosses are critical.

Under all this pressure, myriads of people are working harder and enjoying it less. The huge number of two-income families and single working parents must manage not only their work life but their family life as well. (See step 6.) All this activity and demand can become frustrating and exhausting pretty fast. More and more there is a silent cry from people's souls: *Let me out of here!*

Being a victim does not work. While friends and family afford some succor, the cry for help needs to be directed inward. There is a way out of the dilemma, and it lies within each one of us. Mind Like Water was made for these chaotic times. As usual, we must gird our loins and take a good, hard look at our own thinking. The first examination must be of our hearts. Why do we work? What are we after? Are our goals worthy ones? Have we bought into the false dreams of acquisition and consumption, and are their demands stealing our joy and calmness?

The Misery of Attachment

Why do we run after things? The simplest answer is, we think they will make us happy. But do they produce? Maybe some do. For a little while. If we're lucky. Then it's back to the grindstone, straining and striving after the next thing! Did you ever bend every effort to get something—say, a new car or house—only to have it soon pale into ho-hum insignificance, or even start to become a burden? Some lines from Shakespeare's sonnet on lust—"past reason hunted, past having hated"—could describe any desired thing we go after. Sages of all times have declared that intense striving for future material payoffs never leads to happiness. But do we listen? No; human beings continue to go down those same rat holes, even though they've proved again and again to be empty of cheese.

Granted, we must work just to subsist in the world; we must provide for ourselves and our families. It's not working that must be changed or done away with, but the *way* we work. What is the needed change? What is the way to work that we can still be happy as we go along day to day, short of achieving our goals? Great philosophical and spiritual leaders over time have provided the solution. They say that whereas the usual way of striving after material things—power, possessions, prosperity, etc.—is the source of suffering, we should work so as "not to be attached to the fruits of our labors."

Enjoying the Journey

What does it mean to work unattached? It means that at each moment along the way toward achieving a goal, you are giving your energy, activity, and brainpower fully, *in absolute contentedness with the way things are.* This looks like a contradiction to most people; to them, feeling utterly complete inside is unthinkable, short of completing the project they're working on.

Americans have never enjoyed the journey very much. They just want to get there. That's the cause of the Runaround—the state of distraction and instability so many people are experiencing in these times. People are troubled in their work because they expect to reach their goals in a linear fashion, but they're always being interrupted or sidetracked. With turbulence comes complexity: interruptions and setbacks are occurring frequently, conditions are constantly changing. As a result, few tasks or projects are completed in a straight-on fashion, on time, as originally conceived. In fact, it makes no sense to insist that they be done that way. Many times a shift in conditions will necessitate a change in direction that produces an unanticipated improvement in a product or service.

When we work without attachment to what we're working for and a setback comes along, we're able to say, "Ah, so." In other words, we practice acceptance of what has happened—even while getting busy to fix or change it. That reversal of fortune, which sends the attached person into a tailspin, may throw us momentarily. But it can't get us down; in our state of unhookedness we are "like water." Remember the property of absorption? No matter what object is thrown into a body of water, it responds appropriately. It does not get ready; it does not flinch or react. It merely receives, and returns once again to a placid state.

Dancing on the Rugs

Given that the new condition of the workplace is chaos—rugs coming out from under us more or less continuously—we need to stop slipping and tripping and flopping about, and start ... dancing! When you dance, your weight is never resting more than momentarily on any one point on the floor. You are in motion, and you are enjoying yourself. You are content in the ever-changing nature of your activity. If we are to find satisfaction in the way we are working, we need to lighten up. We must find fun in the work itself.

What if the journey—getting to our goal rather than finally being there—were the whole point of work? What if goals were means rather than ends? One thing is certain: we would find ourselves at home in the Land of Paradox. Luckily for us, we already live there. Working without attachment to outcome is right in keeping with all the other contradictions and absurdities we meet every day.

Mind Like Water Exercises

■ *Take Care of Number One*

Be "unselfishly selfish." Do whatever it takes to be fit, well, rested, conscious, and happy—so you can be fully there, fully available mentally, emotionally, physically, and spiritually, to serve others. Good relationships and satisfying work are matters of *attention control.* You need to balance noise and rushing with peace and quiet. Single working parents need to negotiate alone-time with their kids. (When my own parents went away on vacation they told us, "We'll be better for you when we come back." They were!)

■ *Keep Making Psychic Deposits*
You can't give to others out of an empty emotional bank account. Do things every day that please the real You. Satisfy your emotional needs to be with loved ones and people who make you feel good about yourself.

Satisfy your physical needs by exercise, relaxation, eating well, and getting plenty of sleep. Don't tolerate a stressful minute. Stop and breathe deeply. Do what it takes to bring your mind back to the present. Satisfy your spiritual needs by being alone and seeking the comfort that only the soul knows about. Decide what's important and do that; let the rest go.

■ *Value Your Values*
Integrity causes ripples. People want to be around someone who is true to something. Be willing to share with customers not only what you know but also what's important to you. Walk your talk. Live what you stand for.

■ *Take on Your Futurizing Mind*
Think: "What is it these days I'm so bent on having, so striving to attain? What do I think will make me so happy and satisfied when it happens?" Once you have the answer, let go of it. Work toward your goal, maintaining that same detached state of mind. Experience each moment of the way as being sufficient. When you get to the goal, see that it's just another "moment of is."

■ *Serve Your Customers*
"Customers" are those influenced or affected by you or your actions. This includes not only business clients but also bosses,

gnomes and minions (direct reports), teammates, workmates, spouses, kids, those you teach or coach, etc. In other words, your customers are all the people in your life you take time for and care about. (Of course, you are their customer, as well.)

Concerning your dealings with your customers, there are two remarkably simple and powerful rules:

- Remember that customers get *you*.
- Give them the best *you* they can get.

Why would a growing number of people pay more in a place of business where they feel well served? Why would employees leave a job where they were well paid and take up one in which they are well treated? Why would many parents choose a teacher for their child who is new at the job but pleasant to be around, over an experienced teacher who is cranky and difficult?

In the service business we are all in, most people focus on what is being exchanged—goods, products, information, problem-solving, etc. But beyond the product or service your customers receive, above all else they get *you*. "You" includes everything you are and bring to the point of contact—your level of awareness, honesty, passion, attention, energy, caring, awakeness.

Each individual you deal with can discern (electrically fast, and often without knowing) whatever mood, state of mind, or physical shape you're in, and whatever values you're operating from. Above all, he or she can read how much you *care*—what difference it makes to you that they are there and that they have needs. If you act rushed, distracted, or off-balance, the message to customers is clear: They're in your way.

As shoppers we've all had the demeaning experience of being treated by a service person as if we're an intrusion. We've been subjected to cranked-out, robotic "service." We've ended by deciding we'd do better to get what we need from a book or a computer screen. It costs five times more to get a new customer than to retain an existing one. Save your energy—keep them satisfied.

■ *Value Your Attention as Your Gift*

Attention is like sunshine; it grows and nurtures what it falls upon. When you give full attention to your work, you nurture its perfection. When you give attention to people, they glow with satisfaction at receiving the gift of even a few moments of it. Your customers can read you like a book. Like Santa, they know when you are sleeping, they know when you're awake. "Awakeness" is a key word today because life is moving so fast it can become a blur. It's easy to fall asleep and just *think* you're awake. An out-of-balance server doesn't deliver full service—just as a young child knows the second his or her parent's mind goes south, and says, "You're not listening to me."

Stop thinking, "What's next?" or "That's 145 down, 796 to go!" In fact, stop thinking at all. When you are being fully *with* what is happening *now,* you've got nothing on your mind but that. That's when you are fully present, awake. In fact, that's the only time that counts.

■ *Make Serving Its Own Reward*

There's nothing worse than giving from duty and obligation. Don't keep score of who owes whom. If you find yourself thinking, "Okay, I've done this for them. But what do *I* get out of it? When does *my* turn come?" you've missed the point. Real service is win-win from the get-go. Both your customers and you are energized and fulfilled. Make it fun, create value out of your interactions. Act as if, whenever you're in contact, benefits are automatically flowing both ways.

If you're serving to get something, you're attached to an outcome. You've left the moment. You've left the customer, and he or she will feel your absence.

■ *Learn to Destress*

People in burnout can't serve others. How did they get that way? By not serving themselves, not balancing "What's in it for the customer?" with "What's in it for me?" Breathe. Relax. Meditate. Exercise. Create solitude. Delegate (give others the gift of contributing). Call in well once in a while. A good motto these days is, *If it's not fun, why are you doing it?*

Speaking of fun, SouthWest Airlines, the only consistently profitable company in its industry for the past two decades, has built its reputation on low-cost fares, simplicity of service—and craziness. The lightness and sense of humor that employees bring to customers is legendary. The experience of flying SouthWest is truly different. The air transportation industry is not known for being pleasant—it's known for being grim. Consequently, it's pleasant to be around a team of people who don't take themselves too seriously; the informality, jokes from flight attendants and from the cockpit lighten everybody up. If there is a delay or an inconvenience, it seems less important. Many people will fly only SouthWest, even though it often takes longer to get there, because it's so enjoyable.

■ Don't Do Service "to" People

When you give a customer a solution, you may be taking away his or her ownership of it. Helping people find their own answers works better. Not only does it empower them, it keeps their monkeys off your back. If you're prone to give people answers and solutions, it can come back to bite you. (If your solution doesn't work, whom do they blame? You. If it does work, whom do they call next time for another answer? You.)

Ask for help to get your ego out of the way of the service that wants to be done through you. Think: "I am not the doer, but the instrument of the Doer." (You can make the doer be God, service, positive energy, the life force, or your Higher Power.) You'll be surprised at the energy and vitality you generate and save—and at the joy you'll have—by just a little conscious practice of this ego-removal technique.

Some overly zealous service people fall prey to the disease of rescuing—doing for others what they should be doing for themselves. Some even play the Never Enough game (I never do enough for people!). They can't relax, or say, "That's good enough," or learn to receive from others. Since the only payoff is to die, this view of "service" needs reframing. Reframe your service job—from solving others' problems to facilitating their finding their own solutions. Shift your attention from thinking up answers to guiding people to the correct questions. A powerful strategy is repeating people's ideas back to them, using your own words, so they can hear themselves think.

■ Stop Thinking about What's Next

Typical of the way we "listen" to customers is to be nodding and thinking of what we will say when they finish talking. (Oops! We just lost part of what they said. Maybe it was the most important part!) Whenever your mind wanders into the future and starts trying to control, bring it back. Don't jump to conclusions. Don't assume you know what people need. Don't listen faster than they can talk. Staying present means keeping your balance. It's okay to make plans and set goals; but give up being attached to your notions of how things will turn out. Hold them lightly; then you won't be disappointed if they change or are taken away.

■ See Everyone as a Customer

Whenever you interact with someone, think of that person as a customer. He or she is receiving your attention, your smiles, your stories, your listening. That's service. If you start seeing your spouse, your boss, your friends as your customers, you'll get better at pleasing them. If this is done sincerely, it won't cost you. It will reward you many times over.

■ Be Calmly Active, Actively Calm

Reframing—changing what you are seeing with—is the new mind-elegance tool. By using the tool, you're not thrown when the rug comes out from under you. In the midst of the battle, it's useful to reconceptualize change and one's role, as in:

- This change is not good or bad, it's just what's happening. I can calmly respond to the new situation by letting go of expectations. When I don't hold on to the way it was, but open my mind to the way it is, I stay present and powerful.
- My moment is now. Not in some past or future time, but right here is where all my experience is, all my power to make things happen. Let me do the right thing *now*.
- My new role is change manager. That means paying attention in a new way, handling my own inner states in appropriate response to outer changes.
- I used to be in control; now I'm in power.

Today's working people are faced with the twofold challenge of doing more in less time, while handling unexpected occurrences along the way. Many are fighting their way down the river of their workday or workweek, getting beaten up by the journey. They react by rushing more furiously, trying to gain control. It is this reacting mode, not the outward pace or the duties themselves, that stresses them.

Never "hit the ground running!" Instead, enter this day so as to make sure that when you lie down tonight you've done some of the important things.

> Every day you make a difference in the life of each customer.
> You either make it easier or more difficult.
>
> —BARBARA COULTON-ROBERTS

form-changing

❧

Water can change its form, assuming solid, liquid or gaseous form as conditions demand. In essence, however, it remains H_2O.

Lesson: You can "go with the flow," adapting your behavior as necessary. Throughout all, be anchored from within by your values and mission.

Question Reality

Sometimes you have to look reality in the eye—and deny it.

—GARRISON KEILLOR

Years ago I was facilitating a training session for a large group of teachers. One of the activities was a simulation game in which a purposely confusing problem was posed for their reflection. Assured that there was one correct answer, they were given time to develop their solutions. Their task then was to go out and try to reach consensus around one answer by talking and listening to others. After a lot of argument and trying to convince one another, the game was stopped and the correct answer was given. In the debriefing session that followed, one person said, "I gained lots of converts to my answer, only to find out I was wrong. I'm wondering how many other times I've done that in my life!"

Such self-questioning bears repeating—often. Most of us go through our life of days utterly convinced that the way we are seeing things is the right way, never questioning our perceptions, never standing aside from our point of view. Sages of all ages have called this delusion, sleepwalking, living in a self-perpetuating dream. On the other hand, when we are willing to give up our "sure things" and be guided by some other way we've not used, we remain trainable.

How We Create Our Own Reality

Most of us who regard our own actions as arising from independent choices of our will would be scandalized to know that we act mostly from habit, yet most psychologists agree that it is so. Our beliefs about what is real concerning ourselves, the nature of the world, and our relation to it, drive most of what we do every day. Not only our routine actions but also the decisions we make and the way we respond to unexpected events (which on the surface seem so spontaneous and self-selected) are mapped out for us ahead of time by the nature of our beliefs. Especially at those times when push comes to shove, we can act very robotlike.

A sort of perceptual domino effect is going on all the time inside our heads, which helps us make sense of our world—and at the same time makes our actions almost totally mechanical. The following diagram—which might simply be labeled BFPA to designate the elements of belief, feeling, perception, and action—will demonstrate this:

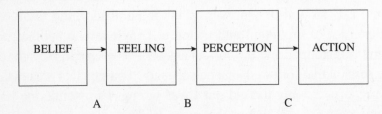

The key points in the diagram are A, B, and C, which break down as follows:

Interaction A: Belief Determines Feeling. What I believe determines the feelings I have toward the matter. For example, if I have a belief that the world is a safe place, I feel safe and confident in it. If I believe that teenagers are unruly and destructive, I will feel wary and distrustful when I'm around people of that age.

Interaction B: Feeling Guides Perception. My feelings, determined by my beliefs, will direct what I choose to notice. I will pay attention to information coming through my senses that reinforces what I already think—and disregard what does not conform to my beliefs. (After all, to acknowledge its existence or to give it any importance would be to question my beliefs. When information and belief clash, information loses.) Ego-mind is always looking to be right. It tells itself again and again, *See? I told you!* (This little self-deception shuffle is built into the very mechanism of perceiving. The only way we can see something is to think it's there, and if we don't think it's there, we can't see it. This truth, which strains at the obvious, explains why love is blind, and also why so many marriages and relationships fail.)

The age-old question between pessimists and optimists is thereby resolved. As to which of them is "right," the answer is: both. They both have data to support their beliefs. What they likely don't realize is that they *started* with the beliefs (or at least long ago bought into them) and currently are just busy reinforcing those points of view by finding data to support them. (Incidentally, I'd rather be the optimist. Optimists may not be totally right, but they have more fun!)

Interaction C: Perception Drives Action. Naturally, my actions flow from the way I look at things. I act out my point of view. If I see my boss as caring genuinely about my ideas, I will submit more and better suggestions and creative ideas for improving things at work. If I see him as critical and uninterested in innovation, I'll keep my ideas to myself, or seek a job where I'm more appreciated.

So What?

There are three conclusions we can draw from the BFPA model:

- The BFPA process is at work during every waking hour, in every human being on the planet.

- People could be dead wrong about what they believe—and very often are.
- By changing their minds—altering their beliefs or substituting new and better beliefs for old—they could powerfully shift their energies in new and interesting directions.

There's bad news and there's good news. The bad news is that all the time those BFPA dominoes are faithfully nudging each other over in my head, creating my reality about a given situation, I could be deluded. The good news about the fact that my beliefs create my reality is that it points to an extraordinary power I have: By changing my beliefs, I automatically change my actions! If my actions can be seen as mechanisms for making be true what I think is true, *why not believe in the best possible things?*

The power to change our minds is what this book is all about. But, you might wonder, how can I change a belief if I believe it? How can I suddenly call into question something that I implicitly think is true? How can I embrace a new belief I've never had before? The answer to all these questions is the same. It is a certain psychic capability, a skill that all of us possess, and that we can greatly strengthen through practice and apply diligently to improve the quality of our lives. The skill is called *reframing*.

Reframing = Re-minding

Reframing is the ability to see something—an object, a person, a situation—in a different way, without changing the outward facts of the matter. It is to shift our conceptual-emotional viewpoint so as to place the situation into another "frame" that fits the situation as well or better. Reframing is deliberately changing your mind, or what might be called "re-minding" yourself. When you can do that at will, you are using the aspect of creativity that is most critical to success in a constantly changing environment.

Something to Practice

Reframing—changing the way you view something—automatically changes your experience of it. Look at the picture below. Do you see a skull?

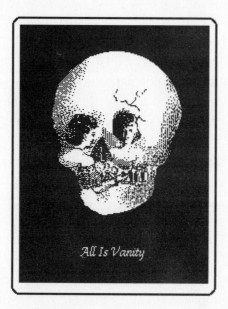

All Is Vanity

Look more closely and see if you can see another picture—a lady at her boudoir mirror. It's a skull—*or* it's a lady. Once you have determined that the picture lends itself to two ways of interpretation, spend a few moments switching back and forth between seeing the picture as a skull and seeing it as a lady. As you do, notice something: *to see the picture one way, you must "let go" of seeing it the other way.* Each time you do this mental letting-go to embrace another perspective, you are reframing—placing the configuration of dark and light spaces on the page into a different mental "frame" of meaning.

Earlier we saw, using the BFPA diagram, that our beliefs determine our attitudes and actions. A corollary of that truth is that *the way we see something determines our attitude toward it.* For example, think of actually having the skull in the room with you, close enough to touch. How would you feel toward it? Repulsed? Disgusted? Next, think of having the woman in your vicinity. If your feelings would be markedly different, you have proved that your view of a thing determines how you feel about it. How would you act in each case, were the skull or the lady close by? What would a videocamera record of your facial expressions, head movements, or gestures? In one case, you might frown or draw away. In the other, you might smile and lean forward. Thus we see again that the way we feel about something determines how we respond to it.

This little experiment demonstrates how reframing something—an object, a situation, a relationship—changes our experience of it. This makes the "skill" of reframing (which, as demonstrated, our brains already know how to do) very powerful and useful. Reframing gets us out of the self-fulfilling trap of ordinary noticing, which operates much as a self-fulfilling prophecy: we see what we expect to see. The ego mind thrives on being right. When you believe a person, place, or thing to be a certain way, your senses scan for what will validate that belief. But when you suspend that belief and look with different eyes, new realities are opened. In short, when you can apply the reframing skill to any situation, you've mastered reality.

Mind Like Water Exercises

■ *Stop Being a Know-It-All*

How is it we so quickly believe that voice inside our heads that assumes it knows what it's talking about? The answer lies in the age-old human addiction to being right—the ego. Proverbs 14:12 of the Bible reads: *There is a way that seemeth right unto a man, but the end thereof is death.* One way to be sure to follow "ways that seemeth right," but aren't, is to be a know-it-all, to assume that you come equipped with superior brain power and infallible knowledge.

I am a know-it-all. Are you? It feels good to admit it. When I'm listening to somebody I often catch myself thinking, "I knew that!" I even think about starting a club called Know-It-Alls Anonymous, whose motto is, "It takes one to know one." When members get together, a conversation around the punch bowl might sound like this:

Ted: (excitedly) I've been thinking a lot about the drawbacks of being a know-it-all, and I've really come up with something!

Mike: Yeah?

Ted: Listen. Do you know what the greatest drawback to being a know-it-all is? (long pause) Well, do you?

Mike: Yep.

Seriously, there are advantages to declaring oneself a know-it-all, one of which is developing humility. The true know-it-all, being omniscient, knows that he or she is addicted to being right. Calling oneself a know-it-all acknowledges this weakness. Don't worry about loss of self-esteem (a know-it-all will not suffer seriously from ego deflation). On the other hand, such an admission triggers humility—a divine quality. (One sage said that God has an inferiority complex—He is great, but He doesn't advertise it.) Practicing *knowing that we don't know* brings us closer to the Truth.

The greatest practical benefit of being a member of Know-It-Alls Anonymous is the opportunity to develop the very trait that members have studiously avoided—a susceptibility to learning new things. It's often said that the most effective organizational leaders are those who, realizing they can be blindsided, are much more excited about what they *don't* know than what they *do.* They encourage followers to explore and make learning mistakes through trial and error. This is what being a "learning organization" is all about.

■ Stop Getting Everything Done

The second most powerful antidote to all the rushing is to examine your beliefs about yourself and tasks. We have seen that without knowing it, we are driven by our thinking about what is so. If we change what we think is so (our reality), our behavioral response automatically changes. One old notion that needs reframing is about *completion*. People are running themselves silly every day because they're still operating on the idea that their job is to "get everything done." It's time to chuck that one on the scrap heap.

It can be a huge relief to get off the getting-it-done treadmill. Since the best way to change a habit is to substitute a new one, a good mantra to start practicing is "I do my best and leave the rest." This shifts the focus from quantity back to quality, where it belongs. Doing your best means being with what you are doing, fully, without fussing about what you haven't done yet.

Another idea left over from the former age of predictability is that things should turn out the way we think. This belief drives people to hold on to their mental pictures of what the end state of their efforts will look like. These days, when change is a way of life, that's a formula for disaster. A good substitute is to develop the aptitude for separating essence from form, and to see that success can always be achieved in a variety of ways. Then, when facing the necessity to modify, you can handle it with ease.

■ *Use Thought Recognition*

Richard Carlson and Joseph Bailey, authors of *Slowing Down to the Speed of Life,* write: "We all have the capacity to call a time-out and recognize our thinking—to see that thought is not an absolute reality but merely our experience of reality in the moment. This process of self-awareness, or thought recognition, is perhaps the most powerful tool we have to restore our mental health."

Whenever we are rushed or stressed or afraid, we can wake ourselves up by recalling *I am thinking this.* The very act of doing that will begin to change our experience. Try it. Next time you're uptight, step aside and acknowledge that you are thinking a certain way, and that that, not outward conditions, is creating your experience of stress.

To "question reality" means to manage the mind's beliefs, and in the process to break up our apparently solid pictures of the world. In the process, we impact our own attitudes and actions. The ability to stand aside and see that we create our own reality is the mark of a master. In this age of unreasoning anxiety, when attention is outward, we can deliberately induce higher states of consciousness by altering our reality. By doing so, we positively affect our own evolution.

Stay Audible-Ready

It's when you're caught surprised or flat-footed that you don't have the time to properly evaluate, and you end up making bad decisions. Shula never let this happen.

—said of Don Shula, former Miami Dolphins head coach

You leave work at lunchtime to catch a break at a café from the hectic train of the morning's events. As you wait for your order, you make a list of things you will do when you get back to the office, prioritizing them carefully so the most important items will be addressed first. Driving back to work, you anticipate getting in there and getting these tasks done—you are even excited about it. But when you reach the office you find that certain changes have taken place while you were absent.

You check your e-mail and find two items that will change your plans. While you are implementing one of these requirements, your boss comes by, hands you a memo, and says, "Drop everything, this is important!"

The boss leaves and as you are reading it, the phone rings. It's an important supplier with a big problem on a critically needed shipment. While you're talking, a fellow employee runs up to tell you your input is need *right now* in a meeting you hadn't planned to attend. And so it goes. But now, imagine that throughout this series of interruptions you have remained placid and unruffled, able to handle each one, choose priorities, and make right decisions each time. You could do so with Mind Like Water!

Whatever you call them—surprises, unanticipated events, accidents, interruptions—it's our reactions to these everyday sudden turns in the maze that we must learn to use to develop a skill just about everybody these days is in need of. It's the ability to stop what you're doing, withdraw attention completely from it, and focus elsewhere—with absolutely no leftovers of resentment or frustration. In football, that's known as being audible-ready.

An article in a recent issue of *Fast Company* magazine said that the average worker in America experiences 6 interruptions every hour. It cataloged the average number of messages received in a day: 52 phone calls, 3 cell-phone calls, 36 e-mails, 23 voice mails, 18 postal items, 18 office memos, 13 Post-its, 8 hard copies, 3 express mails, and 14 faxes. Being audible-ready is also important to winning in your life and work. It's good to start out with a plan, but it's advisable to hold it lightly, ready to let go of your mental picture of how things would transpire without regret when conditions warrant doing so. Training our minds to handle change fluidly cannot be done except in the school of daily life. We don't have to worry about not getting a proper workout each day though handling jarring, unanticipated changes. Inevitably they will come at us. Each one will arrive unannounced as if to say, "Here I am, to disrupt your plans. Now what are you going to do about me?"

The quarterback calls a play in the huddle. The team lines up. The QB looks at the other team, notices their defense is set up in a way that will block the chosen play, so he calls an "audible"—announces numbers that signal an alternate play. In the next few seconds, each listening player must mentally let go of what he was about to do and get ready to carry out a new and different assignment.

This team has been set up from the beginning to be audible-ready—that is, to operate with the capacity to switch plays on a dime. They'd better be: imagine a player who comes out of the huddle thinking of what he's to do in the called play, then when he hears the audible—the signal to change horses in midstream—he says, "Hey, I liked that other play. Why do I have to change? I'm just going to carry out the assignment I was planning to do!"

There's no point in holding to a game plan that isn't working. When he coached the Miami Dolphins to their 1972 perfect season and eventually to back-to-back Super Bowl victories, Don Shula worked on preparation for the unexpected like a field general commanding his troops. He was always asking, "What if ... ?" so that when a change occurred, he and his players weren't caught flat-footed.

Preparing for Eventualities

The key to being adaptable is to be prepared in the first place. Audibles are not last-minute orders the quarterback has dreamed up out of nowhere. They are strategies the players are familiar with and have practiced beforehand. They are *new ways of doing what you already know how to do.* This definition of audibles is most useful in developing Mind Like Water.

In his book *Managing as a Performing Art,* Peter Vaille compares the turbulence felt in the business environment these days to a roaring river. He says we must all learn how to live in "perpetual white water." After the publication of *What's the Rush?,* I developed a training design for follow-up seminars in applying the skills of the book. In the process of fitting Vaille's metaphor of white water change to the work sector, I consulted with world-class kayakers to find out how the things they experienced could be applied to dealing with churning change. By listening to their descriptions, and by studying video footage of expert paddlers working in the toughest of conditions, I found some extraordinary applications to living in the white water of constant change.

Embedded in the experts' accounts of their subjective experiences were many hints of Mind Like Water. I quote one such account here, by world-class kayaker Eric Magnuson:

The moment before you drop into a big rapid, your concentration is absolute. Any fear or doubt there once was is gone. There's just no room for it. Sitting in a kayak you're only three feet high, and the waves around you are pretty big, so it's really hard to see what's going on. You're trying to pull off a series of precise moves to be in pretty exact spots in the rapid. Time warps. Sometimes it seems to slow and stretch, and things seem crystal clear. Then other times everything's flashing by in fast-forward, and you're just straining to keep it all together. You don't have to think about what your body is doing; it seems to respond instinctively. It's a total mind-body experience.

Eric's words about trying to "pull off a series of precise moves" describe what most of us are trying to do every day, particularly when pressure builds up at work, as do those about "straining to keep it all together." The key to operating effectively (meaning both successfully and with satisfaction) is found in those last sentences, which describe a noncognitive, instinctive response. That is, Mind Like Water.

The so-called extreme sports, such as taking on dangerous rivers in a kayak or rock-climbing a sheer thousand-foot face, are instructional of intuitive functioning. Oftentimes there is no time to think, so the participant must operate "out of her head." As such, they may provide models for doing the work we do in these speeded-up times, without much of the analysis and deliberation to which we're accustomed.

Mind Like Water Exercises

■ *Let Your Body Choose*

Thomas J. Leonard, author of *The Portable Coach,* writes: "As a certified financial planner ... I added up every possible variable so I could make the right decision in every situation.... I'd list all the pros and cons, weigh the odds, consider the short- and long-term consequences, and—eventually—I would make up my mind. One day I started to realize something very alarming. My decisions were rarely the best ones.... So, instead of relying exclusively on my mind to make decisions and choices, I started letting my *body* choose for me."

Most of us somehow know that if we could learn to trust ourselves to let our bodies—our gut feelings—make decisions for us, they would be the right ones. The problem is that we are so used to living "in our heads" that we don't know how to entrust our minds to another way.

■ Dip on the Crest

As I viewed footage of expert river-runners, I noted that often when a kayaker was literally out of sight behind mountains of roiling water, upon emerging he would be relaxed and alert. As his boat rose from the trough, he might dip his paddle to maintain direction, but the effort was minimal. My friends told me that it is useless for the paddler to try to make a difference when he is down in the trough between waves, as the boat ends are buried in water. Conversely, when he's on the crest of the wave the boat ends are out; one little dip can make the needed horizontal difference in direction.

In the same way, when we are buried in a problem and can't see the way out, it is futile to thrash about, wildly seeking solutions. That's the time to relax and watch. When we are up on top, able to see where we are going, that's the time to look for a chance. As soon as opportunity flashes among the turbulence, we are ready to dip our paddle.

■ Give Up Expecting

A major difficulty in handling rapid change is letting go of how we *expect* something to be, in order to be with it the way it actually is. The essence of applied creativity today is connected to the skill of *reframing* (see step 13). To be able to handle sudden setbacks and disappointments with minimum effort, we must first look at how invested we are in our outcomes.

The way to enter the flow of mindless mind/timeless time is to let go of expectations. The dictionary defines expectation as "a looking forward to, as due, proper, or necessary." The setup point for dissatisfaction is a previous expectation, a mental picture of how things should look when we get where we're going. When our hopes are dashed, the tendency is to blame people or other forces that play a part in the outcome. In reality we should be taking responsibility for having set ourselves up for the letdown in the first place. Thus, *the way to avoid being disappointed is not to expect anything in the first place.*

■ Hold Goals Lightly

Expectations play such a prominent role in the Runaround that most people would find it difficult to think of living without them, but they would be far better off to do so. This doesn't mean we shouldn't set goals, or strive to achieve them. It means we should do so with a detached attitude. What does it mean to be detached? It means concentrating one-pointedly on performing our work in a manner that satisfies our need for quality and artistic joy, trusting the outcome wholeheartedly to the future.

There is a natural flow of events that can be thought of as a flow of water, a natural stream. The irony is that if we jump out of the flow, trying to anticipate a future part of the stream by being at a different place in it than we are, when we finally do arrive at the anticipated point we will not be able to enjoy it or be with it, for we will have trained our mind to "futurize." Conversely, by focusing on the here and now, where we actually are in the flow, and by avoiding thinking about what is to come, we can bring our energy and creativity to the moment, and experience joy at each point along the river's way.

■ Reframe Interruptions

Recognize that the entire experience of what you call "being interrupted" needs to be reframed away from association with tension, disappointment, and frustration. Think of each surprise as an opportunity rather than an obstruction.

■ *Stand Aside*

Watch yourself when things occur to change what you expected to happen. Note the resistance you have to the way events turned out; let go of it so you can determine what to do. Perhaps you need not change plans. Perhaps you need to. Put yourself in a place where you can hold both options and freely select the right one.

■ *Think, "What If?"*

Whenever you make a plan or set a goal, don't cast it in cement. In order not to be caught flat-footed, create a backup, a contingency plan. Plan Bs, especially if they're well thought out and choreographed ahead of time, often work out better. So much is beyond your control that sometimes you have to change not just your play but your whole game plan.

■ *Build New Skill Sets*

The fluctuating economy is teaching many investors the need for flexibility. Cross-training in companies helps ensure against loss of people, in that others can step into a job or task when needed. We need to teach our minds to imagine personal "recessions" and to "cross-train" ourselves, accepting new ways of thinking and behaving that may seem uncomfortable at first.

■ *Don't Always Zig, Sometimes Zag*

Every day cut new grooves in the brain by taking some small action that "isn't you." Choose something you don't usually do—brushing your teeth with the opposite hand, taking a different route to work, parking on the opposite side of the lot, watching an unlikely show, or reading a book of a different genre.

■ *Practice Mental Relaxation*

Mental relaxation is a skill; in these turbulent times it might even be called an art form. Those of us with habitually busy, restless, on-the-go states of mind should consider adopting the deliberate practice of mental relaxation. What is it? *Mental relaxation is the ability, at will and at any time, to free the attention from nagging worries and present and past difficulties.*

■ Have Nothing on Your Mind, and Be Proud of It

When I was a teenager and we went to Cape Cod in the summer, my siblings and I would have a race to see who could achieve the mental state we called "Caped." It was a condition in which one had absolutely nothing on one's mind. To this day my brother and I dispute our younger sister's claim to have become Caped one summer while crossing the Bourne bridge on the drive down.

People have so much on their minds these days, it's easy to forget who put it all there. We were not made for worries; they were made by us. The more plagued and fretted with worries our minds are, the less we'll be able to recognize an opportunity for changing horses. An important part of being audible-ready—of going with the aquanamous flow—is ridding ourselves of unnecessary mental burdens. We should not allow them to torture us.

■ Give Up Your Plan

As with individuals, so with their organizations. Most companies today are finding that a fixed game plan or published organizational chart no longer suits their operation. It's the companies that are constantly adapting themselves to new conditions—changes in markets, economy, customer base, technology—that are making the most striking advances. For the past few years, articles on developing intuition have appeared in business magazines. Today's profile of an effective business leader includes reliance on gut instinct.

Richard Bode, author of *First You Have to Sail a Little Boat*, points out that often in sailing the shortest distance between two points is a zigzag line. "Each separate tack calls for a major readjustment ... if the maneuver is handled fluently, the boat continues to surge ahead with a minimum loss of momentum. In due course we arrive, if it can be said that we ever fully arrive. The truth is that there are destinations beyond destinations, and so the confirmed sailor goes on tacking forever."

We are all navigators in the waters of turbulent change. With all the change coming at us, it is up to us to be adaptable, as soft and absorbent in mind as water itself. By developing our ability to tack, to change course appropriately, we shall in due course arrive where we are headed.

STEP 15

Don't Be Difficult

Did you ever notice, when your life isn't working, who's always around?

—Werner Erhard

Everyone has to deal from time to time with difficult people. You know the ones I mean: they're so hard to get along with, they tax your patience and self-control to the limits. Sometimes they act like they just have it in for you. It's as if they've gotten up that morning, looked in the mirror, and said to themselves, "I'm going out there and ruining someone's day." The good news is, there are definite steps you can take to deal with these difficult people. The bad news is, the first and most important step is to make sure you're not one of them.

There was a saint who said: "The basis of right human behavior is self-reform. We should always try to overcome inharmony by display of the best that is in us." You might think, *Well, that's all very well for him to say—he's a saint!* But what is a saint? I like the definition given by Paramahansa Yogananda: "A saint is a sinner who never gave up." When saints talk about bad behavior, they're speaking from experience. The advice of the one I quoted is echoed by a principle often taught in management courses: *If you want to know the cause of most difficulties in your relationships, go look in a mirror.*

Responding Well

Self-reform means self-control—controlling our feelings and words and reactions. It's very easy to get riled up under pressure, when somebody blames or insults you, or otherwise treats you badly. But regardless of what the other person does, the response you make is the deciding factor in whether the situation heats up or cools down.

Person A is under pressure, frustrated or angry, and lets fly with a choice remark toward Person B. Person B's response in this situation is the key. If B smiles or uses understanding and sweet words, we have no argument. But if B takes the remark personally and reacts in kind, now we have *two* upset people. That's the beginning of an episode that will be regretted later.

I frequently have this problem with a person I know who has a unique ability to push all my buttons. I like him, but I find myself frustrated and blaming whenever he does or says certain things. The trouble is, when I go away and reflect and analyze the situation, it always turns out that—darn it! It was *my reacting* to his moods and words that produced the trouble. If it just weren't for those buttons!

Mind Like Water Exercises

■ *Use Silence*

That same saint used to say: "Fools argue; wise people discuss." In potentially ugly situations, you always have the choice to remain silent and run the chance of looking like a fool—or to open your mouth and remove all doubt. The tongue may become sore or numb from prolonged holding, but that's better than—well, you know.

■ *Maybe You're Right*

When receiving harsh words, take them in and think, *Maybe there's some truth in what this person is saying, albeit in a not-very-nice way.* Then outwardly respond by saying sincerely, "Maybe you're right." (If sincerity is in question, you could fake it till you make it on this one; just keep eye contact and patiently repeat, "Maybe you're right. Maybe you're right," until they're out of gas.) Showing genuine interest and repeating back what they said, while difficult, can be disarming. "Let's see, you're ticked off because thus-and-so. Is that right?"

■ *Prior Reflection*

You can't know when a potentially ugly confrontation will arise, but you can arm yourself through anticipating and self-questioning. Ask: Do I have a need to be right? When do I let pride get in the way? Am I able to cut off my speech at any time? What are the warning signs when anger or impatience is starting to control me? What are my buttons? Should I remain quiet when I'm attacked—or should I clear the area and let the other person cool off?

■ *The Power of Prayer*

Get quiet and give it all away. A good petition (but one that raises the difficulty level) is: "Change no circumstance of my life, change me."

Your good example will do more to change others than many words, wrath, or just wishing. As you improve yourself, you will elevate the consciousness of others around you.

Carry an imaginary mirror with you today.

Stop every now and then, and check yourself in it.

motivelessness

❧

Water has no agenda of its own.
It has nothing to prove.
It fits and flows around things,
taking its shape from its environment.

Lesson: *Let go of your needs and plans. Trust that by watching and waiting, and by doing your best, your needs will be provided for.*

STEP 16

Be a Time Millionaire

If by eternity is understood not endless temporal duration but time-lessness, then he lives in eternity who lives in the present.

—LUDWIG WITTGENSTEIN

There is widespread "time famine" in the world. People are suffering because of lack, not only of food or water, but of time. The frequently heard complaint "I never have enough time!" points to a shared perception that leads to a pervasive cultural anxiety. Time scarcity, while it is a source of great suffering for people, also points to a great possibility. *By changing our ideas about time, we can have much more of it.*

We could approach the time problem from an entirely analytical point of view. We could say that each of us has exactly the number of hours in a day or a week as a person in prison, a paraplegic in a hospital, or a monk in a Zen monastery. We just choose to spend ours differently. But does this approach help us? Does it change our thinking? No. To do that, we must examine our beliefs about time. Remember the BFPA model that shows how beliefs drive feelings, perceptions, and actions? Nowhere is that perceptual system harder at work keeping "reality" in place than with regard to time.

What is time? Like the workings of the human body, the aspect of the world we call time is elusive to explanation, yet, as with our bodies, most of us take time for granted. Though there is a shared meaning, a social definition of time as linear, as measured by the clock, each of us has a different perspective, a slightly different definition of himself or herself and the world, within which the notion of time is fixed. Great thinkers such as Einstein, Jung, Kant, and Ouspensky have agreed that time is essentially a property of consciousness, that the idea of time arises through the knowledge of the world that comes to us through our senses. They say that the so-called time-sense is the sensation of changing moments.

Take a minute to think about what time means to you. Is it the same as aging? Is it based on how long you have lived or how long before you might die? Is it an actual thing, something that can be cut up into pieces and measured, or does it exist only in the mind? What about those experiences—among them the most transcendent in life—when time seems to go away? Do the normal shared assumptions about time explain moments of serendipity or déjà vu? Your responses to these questions will demonstrate that time is subjective, and that your "take" on it is entirely your own.

Imagining Timeless Time

Westerners tend to perceive time as linear, but there are other views of time. P. D. Ouspensky, a Russian writer and experimenter with perception, reached outside of our neatly constructed framework of linear time when he wrote: "In time 'events' exist before our consciousness has touched them, and they still exist after our consciousness has left them." He's saying that everything already exists, but it is being tracked by our brains only moment by moment. If he's right, it's small wonder that mystics and sages speak of the experience of cosmic consciousness as disorienting; rather than its accustomed habit of meting out momentary drops of time, the mind is suddenly flooded with the entire ocean of Now.

Normal waking consciousness never rises above a definite plane. But what if it could? Just as when gazing down from the top of a mountain you can see two different cities that at ground level are hidden from each other, why could it not be that, rising above your "normal" plane of consciousness, you could see simultaneously events normally separated by time? The angle of vision will enlarge during such an ascent. The moment will expand. If you imagine your receptivity on a plane higher than your consciousness, you will understand the concept of being able to "grasp eternity." It is to experience all that is happening for you during a length of time (minutes, hours, a day, a month) as *simultaneous*. You would not be able in such a heightened state to discriminate among *before, now,* or *after.* All would be Now.

Schopenhauer declared, "It is always a sign of genius to treat difficult matters simply." Historically, the measure of creativity has been the ability to see something that others have not seen. These days the ability to see something in a way you have never seen it before is perhaps an even greater measure of creative ability. We can't add more hours to the day, but the effect is the same when we work to change our ideas about time. If we can find a way to deliberately change the way we view time we will *automatically change the way we experience it.*

Detachment Is the Key

What makes reframing difficult is attachment. As demonstrated, you can't place a person, situation, or object into a new conceptual "frame" without letting go of the old way of conceptualizing him, her, or it. Reframing requires you to give up the way things used to appear to you. Actually, this ability to come unstuck from one's former ideas in order to reconceptualize a thing is in high demand in competitive arenas, where strategy counts—business, sports, war. (For a decade now, business leaders have been told that one of the most useful questions they can ask is, "What business are we really in?" This is a call for reframing on an organizational level. Redoing the conceptual structure of a firm's business requires self-discipline and courage. Leaders who have accomplished this have been hailed for the past few years as the most innovative and flexible—in other words, the most creative.)

Mind Like Water Exercises

■ *Embrace the Present*

Thomas J. Leonard, writer and founder of Coach University, says, "When you recognize and accept that things are the way they are, and that the present is all we truly have, then it's not too much of a leap to believe that the present is perfect. Maybe it's not optimum, but it is perfect to learn from and perfect to grow from. The present is all you have, and it is your point of power, the only place you have to do things from, to initiate, to make changes, to make things happen. Only in the present are you empowered."

The past is history, the future is mystery, but this moment is a gift; that's why they call it the present. This popular saying captures the notion that the present is all we really have, and that whatever it holds for us, it portends our best.

■ *Practice Abundance*

Here are two extremely important assumptions to consider:

■ Nothing happens by accident.

■ The universe means us no harm.

Like other beliefs, these assumptions are self-fulfilling. Once you buy into them, and especially as you begin to bank on them in the way you live your life, you will see that every day they "come true." Taken together, these statements comprise a reality of abundance. Patience may be required; sometimes you have to wait for the proof, but it will always show up. By relying on these as truths as the moral basis of reality, you can do what it takes to live happily amid uncertainty. This outlook does not rely on circumstances or conditions for its strength; it automatically assumes that "all things work together for good." It does not deny evil or misfortune, it looks beyond it.

Numerous studies have shown that people with a positive outlook on life suffer far less sickness than those who see the world in negative terms. The former also have more energy. To exercise innate trust with your world if you are not already blessed with it, you need more than belief; you need a change of heart. Unbeknownst to you, you have been searching out and anticipating the bad things. They are assuredly there, but the point is that you see them because you're looking for them. Remember the reframing you did with the skull-or-lady picture? Experimentation is in order: you need to change what you are seeing with.

■ *Practice Contentment*

One of the first ways you can see that the universe is basically benevolent is to practice contentment. Instead of having what you want, start *wanting what you have.* Wanting—accepting fully— what you already have is the basis for enlightened and empowered action in the present. Perhaps what you have is unavoidable, unpleasant, even painful, and you have tended to avoid it. As you choose to go through that acceptance gate, you will be more likely to deal responsibly with unwelcome tasks and situations in the future, rather than avoiding them.

■ *Act "As If"*

The idea that our true experience occurs timelessly, outside of what we think of as measured time, can produce a change for us if we act as if it is true. Acting this way—timelessly—automatically makes us time-rich. It's as if there is only Now, just this one infinite moment, in which to live. This in no way negates or cripples our ability to deal with clock time, to make plans and keep appointments. It just means we recognize that we are doing what all people do who "keep time"—we are acting in accordance with recognized agreements. Thus we can keep time within the infinite present. Far from being in opposition to the notion of timeless existence, clock time is understood to be subsumed by it.

■ Go by Body Time

The circadian rhythms by which plants, animals, and young children live suggest that "body time" is more natural, more *real,* than "clock time." When we are run solely by clock time we lose much of the joy and vitality waiting to be tapped in each waking moment. Our spontaneity and creativity are generated outside of measurable time; by visiting there we gain ideas and products to be used within real time. We can view time and space as they come to us in the form of experiences, and relationships.

■ Value Timeless Things More

Revisit your aspirations, dreams, and hopes regularly. Observe the perpetual current of thoughts and emotions that arise within you. Life is manifesting itself richly in all these ways, to all of which clock time is totally irrelevant.

■ Live Life as It Comes Up

By the practice of being fully in each moment we discover that we don't need to know things beforehand. We can be so open to the present that we don't have to work out mentally what happens next. We can transcend that way of thinking—splitting our attention by escaping from the moment, creating contingencies, etc.—altogether. How beautiful and fulfilling life becomes when you are not waiting for the next moment!

■ *Become Time-Rich*

What if, right amid all the rush and bustle of our days, we could literally have all the time in the world? Guess what? We do. Assume that at any given moment you have all the time in the world—that is, you have all the time you need to do what you should be doing. What would you do—feel, act like—if you were convinced you had all the time in the world? The answers are plain. You'd feel calm, focused, imperturbable, fearless, absorbed, relentless. Your performance would improve dramatically. Whatever you were doing would be done better, and in less time, because of your concentration. When others around you were losing their heads, they'd need only look and see that you still had yours.

■ *Use the Affirmation*

I came across the time-rich concept at the most unlikely moment—when I was rushing to an important meeting in my car. I'd been held up, and was concerned about being late. As I was frustratedly blaming the traffic, cursing red lights, and tailgating the car in front of me, the phrase suddenly popped into my head and I said aloud, "I am a time millionaire." Instantly my shoulders relaxed, my hands stopped gripping the wheel, and my face lighted up with a big grin. Just thinking of that phrase seemed to endow me with all the time I needed. I stopped rushing and started blessing Paramahansa Yogananda for his phrase "smile millionaire," which had cued my response. (Naturally, when I reached my destination the person I was to meet hadn't arrived yet.)

■ *Use Feelings*

As a means of avoiding the time famine from which most of society sees itself as suffering, it's useful to repeat the affirmation "I am a time millionaire" as often as you can remember to do it. By evoking enjoyable feelings of prosperity and plenty, this phrase can relax your mind and focus your attention. Whenever you are rushed, repeat the words a number of times, concentrating on the feelings associated with being a "millionaire."

■ *Fake It Till You Make It*

If you don't buy in immediately to being time-rich, be willing to practice the consciousness of it anyway. Once you begin to see that most of your ideas are exchangeable because you created or bought into them in the first place, you need not question the advisability of giving a new belief a "try-on." Be like my friend Del, who, when I suggested he say aloud "I am a time millionaire" when he's feeling stressed, replied, "But what if I don't believe it?" I countered with, "It doesn't matter. Just say it. Fake it till you make it." He nodded, then suddenly smiled and said, "How about a time *bill*ionaire? We knock you mere millionaires out of the water!" We both laughed.

Being ridiculously time-rich is nothing to be ponderous about. The ego mind, accustomed to thousands of repetitions to itself of a contradicting belief, will likely be scandalized at such a phrase at first. Just tell it to go sit in the corner, and get back to enjoying your wealth. You might even consider those who rush frantically about as the "time-poor of the world." Experiment with the affirmation over time to discover what results it brings. Go on reinforcing the concept. Remember, it has taken you many repetitions of the opposite sorts of phrases to develop a strong belief in time-poverty. Fake it till you make it.

■ *Don't Manage Time*

"The problem with time management," writes Richard Eyre in *Spiritual Serendipity,* "is that time is like tides or currents.... It is far better to learn attitudes that help us use time and flow with it than techniques for trying to manage it." As you work from a time-rich instead of a time-famished base, you'll get far more done in less time—and enjoy it more. Write down and keep handy quotes that remind you that time is not a taskmaster. Make up time-prosperous affirmations and repeat them often. Sample: "I have all the time in the world to do the right thing I need to do."

■ *View the Present from the Future*

Reflecting on past experience gives insight and meaning to it. We look back on things and say, "If I'd only known!" Why can't we do that now, without waiting? I use running as a laboratory for playing around with my own beliefs and perceptions. One of the most powerful "recipes for the sole" I discovered in my mind experiments was *remembering now*—seeing the present moment as a memory. Whatever's happening to you right now is going to be some "past" to a future yourself. So why not invest it *as you live it* with all of the potent meaning and significance it might turn out to have?

For me, remembering now opens immediate possibilities for me. It wakes me up to the potency of the moment I am in. "Well," I think, "if I really do find myself at some future time looking back on this moment as a time that things started to happen, what could have occurred in the interim that would cause me to do that?"

The best thing about this strategy of "remembering now" is that it frees our minds of the drudgery of clock time. Even a few moments' practice of looking back from the future transforms petty pace into the stuff of dreams. And why couldn't you go on into future moments with that same "historic" feeling?

The way to empower ourselves is to dwell in the moment. That's because the present moment is where everything happens. The more we live in it, the more we see that time is not a taskmaster but a vast resource. One of the most powerful ways we can benefit our minds is by playing with our ideas about time. This requires detachment, and the willingness to release the past and the future and *just be here*. When we are fully present, we automatically have all the time in the world.

Call Your Mother

Nature's peace will flow into you as the sunshine flows into trees while cares will drop off like autumn leaves.

—JOHN MUIR

I always felt protected when as a young boy I hiked the forests, climbed the trees, and waded or skated the ponds and streams that surrounded my New England village. My intuitive connection with the natural world—its beauty and tenderness as well as its frightening stormy flashes—seemed an extension of the safety and security I associated with home. When I gazed up into the fathomless vault of a night sky glittering with stars, the wonder and peace that went through me echoed the orderly, nurturing aspect of my family. Deeply I felt it in every part of me: I was safe, I was known, I was loved.

Dangers of Disconnect

A man sits in gridlock traffic. He momentarily glances across the six-lane highway at a meadow with some wooded hills beyond. He looks at the sun sparkling on the water of the river under the nearby overpass. But he does not see these things; his mind is on getting to an appointment at his workplace. His car window is open, but he does not feel the sun's warmth on his arm. He does not hear the song of the bird in the field, or note the wildflowers bending in a breeze. Instead, smelling the exhaust fumes, he rolls up the window, switches on the radio, and activates the air conditioner.

Our coddled existence, if we let it, withholds from us the delicious value of doing for ourselves in the out-of-doors, and blinds us to its natural beauty. The deep, intuitive sense of belonging to and being one with all of Nature, for which there is no substitute, must be cultivated by those whose lives are permeated with instant gratification and artificial everything. When our link with the elements is weakened, we lose touch with the primordial Child who lives within each of us. No longer do we hear that maternal call. We cannot feel our home. We are spiritually lost.

Mother and Child Reunion

The song "Mother and Child Reunion" by Paul Simon extolled an elemental relationship, an essential returning back to ourselves, to the earth where our bodies came from. The 1960s, the era out of which it came, saw a movement in young people to go "back to the land." It was by no means the first such attempt.

Ever since Americans began their move to the cities in the late nineteenth century, each generation has bemoaned the loss of the simpler, more natural processes once associated with life on the farm. The beginning of the Industrial Age saw various back-to-nature movements, communes, and Utopian communities. Fueled by the conviction that in humans beings' relationship with the natural world lies their freedom and fulfillment, people were attempting to salvage something primordial and precious that the bustle and grime of city life were leaching away from the feeling of being human.

As inhabitants of this troubled world, we hold an obligation to restore that feeling, to right the imbalance that our technologically based lifestyle has produced. People and nations who think they must solve their problems by intellectual, mechanical means forget that if they are in tune, they will know what to do. For most of us the main need is just to spend more time out-of-doors, to take ourselves away, sit ourselves down, and let the Mother-and-Child communion take place. The urge is still in each of us, waiting. We need not so much call our Mother as answer her call.

The Key: Receptivity

Answering to the wild, learning from it, letting it change and bless us—all that is quite different from the typical American approach. From the pioneers came the value of overcoming, conquering, placing the land in submission. Out of those early conquests a common arrogance developed toward the natural world, a shared belief that wildlife is to be tamed, observed from a distance, or made a display of. But there were others—Henry Thoreau, John Muir, and Ansel Adams among them—who saw things in a different way.

I didn't grow up around boats, but in later life I am learning to sail. Always a lover of water, I have no interest in motorized craft—kayaks, canoes, and rowboats are my speed. But best of all is sailing. For some years I had constructed small sailing boat models, each built from the keel up the way the real wooden workboats have long been constructed in Maine. Finally I bought a fourteen-foot sailing dinghy and enrolled in a seamanship course.

Many writers have tried to evoke the feeling of maneuvering a small boat in conjunction with the play of the wind. There is nothing like the exhilaration—with just a dash of danger—of hearing the bow wave splash and feeling the tug of the tiller as the boat picks up in a fresh breeze and starts to move. From the joy of sailing comes the wonder of cooperating with the divine breath and letting it take me.

Mind Like Water Exercises

■ *Get Away*

It is possible, and also a good idea, to think of being out in nature as an essential supply to your health and well-being, as vital as air or food. It also well may be that your most creative ideas will dawn on you when you are in the open air. As an example, poet Edward Carpenter, an English contemporary of Walt Whitman, described the process of writing in his famous book of inspired writings, *Towards Democracy.*

The entire book was written in a certain mood that

> has been the sun to which all the images and conceptions and thought used have been as material objects reflecting its light. And perhaps this connects itself with the fact that it has been so necessary to write in the open air. The more universal feeling which I sought to convey refused itself from me within doors. This fact of the necessity of open air is very curious, and I cannot really explain it. I only know that it is so, quite indubitable and insurmountable. I can feel it at once, the difference, in merely passing through a doorway—but I cannot explain it. Always especially the *sky* seemed to contain for me the key, the inspiration; the sight of it more than anything gave what I wanted (sometimes like a veritable lightning-flash coming down from it onto my paper—I a mere witness, but agitated with strange transports).

Whether we are poets or not, Carpenter's analysis of his mystical mood suggests that the open air may be an important component of achieving expression of the unique music each of us has come to make. Perhaps in order to rise to the heights of our best ideas we must leave the accustomed sights and sounds of household and workplace, and take ourselves away to places where the Voice inside us can be heard.

■ *Cultivate Wonder*

Find joy in the everyday things around you. Take time, as they say, to smell the daises (the smell is nice, but the time-taking is what's important). Feel within yourself the subtle change of the seasons. Look at a seashell. Look into a dog's eyes. Stand under a tree and listen to see if it's speaking. Go wading in a creek. Spend time watching a small child at play. Create cloud pictures. Forget what things are called, or why something happens. Get out of your head for a while and don't come back until you are calm and feeling *at-one-ment*.

■ *Keep a Garden*

Some gardeners I know have a feeling about getting out and digging in the earth that I associate with an experience I have had repeatedly as a runner. Taken up with other matters, I might go several days without being out. Then would come that irresistible yearning, that need I could not but answer. Pulling on my running shoes, I would burst away with an immense feeling of relief—*Ah, this! This is what I have needed all along!*

In English villages, where there is little room and where every space is seemingly used, most residents have been careful to cultivate their tiny backyards. With high walls around them and the sun slanting down on a Sunday afternoon in spring, thousands of people will be seen digging and planting and weeding and cultivating narrow beds and strips of soil. They are appreciating what they have been given of the earth, glorying in nature as if they are in the very wilds.

■ *Get an Indoor Fountain and Some Houseplants*

You can create a small arboretum, a nature space, right within your home. Get a small, trickling fountain with an electric pump. Surround it with houseplants, placing some sprigs of ivy or ferns in the water itself. Let the sound of the water remind you of your kinship with all growing things.

■ *Keep a Pet*

Animal friends are a way to keep in touch with the basics. Some people are more open to different levels of communication with animals and plants. You can train yourself to be the same. Treat your pet kindly, being careful to acknowledge in all possible ways what he or she does for you. Great understanding and delight can come to you concerning the capabilities of your pet and of all animals through reading *Kinship with All Life* by J. Allen Boone. Another enlightening book is *The Secret Life of Plants* by Peter Tompkins and Christopher Bird.

■ *Unclutter Your House and Life*

Thoreau said, "A man's wealth consists in the number of things he can leave alone." Cultivate that wealth for yourself by judicious downsizing. Go through an area of your house—perhaps only a cluttered drawer or trunk at first—and clean it out. Throw away everything you've kept because "you might need it someday." (You didn't need it.) Enjoy the feeling of simplicity and space you've gained. Graduate to decluttering a closet or garage or basement. Let the air in. Feel the sense of expansiveness. Make room for new life.

■ *Read Children's Books*

I know adults who, like their children, couldn't wait for the next Harry Potter book to come out. That's because we don't grow up, we just get taller. Reread old classics like *Wind in the Willows* and *Charlotte's Web*. Recapture the innocence and wonder such stories convey. Parents who read much to their children are mistaken to think they are doing the giving. When did you watch *The Wizard of Oz* with tots and not become one?

■ *Take the Long Way Home*

My hometown of Amherst, Massachusetts, is squarely in the center of New England. In every direction there are innumerable journeys to be taken, an endless variety of vistas to be seen. Every so often throughout the turning seasons of the year I start out one morning to perform my routines and take care of business as planned—and sometime in the midmorning I notice it is *that kind of a day*. I look around. No one is watching. I'm on my own. I go quickly and pack a small bag. Soon I am poring over maps or accessing a bed-and-breakfast web site. I choose a road I've never traveled before. If it requires a highway to get away a bit, I soon abandon that wide road for the back ways. I am on a ramble!

Roam away occasionally and get lost. Let your eyes and nose and ears and skin be receptive to new and different places. If you are not your own boss and your time is constricted, it doesn't mean you don't deserve or can't occasionally afford the joys of a vagabond. At least once a week start out a bit earlier from home or work and take some back road that leads you momentarily aside from the boringly known. Note how your spirit feels more refreshed if you wander about a bit before arriving where you were going.

■ *Relive Your Youth*

People often yearn for their childhood days. They miss the simplicity, the freedom from cloying appointments and responsibilities that fill their lives. They sense that back then they knew something worth knowing. Remember what a childhood day was like? If a grownup stopped you on your way out to play and asked you where you were going or what you were going to do, the question seemed irrelevant. You had no plans. You went to *discover* where you were going. It was an adventure—a time when you didn't know what would happen, but you had to go to find out.

Too soon those halcyon childhood years are fled. But did they steal forever your spontaneity? Your sense of wonder? Your ever-new instinctual vitality? The timeless abandon you felt roaming the wilds? And if you didn't have a happy childhood, is it too late to have one? Recall that life is a dream—it is whatever you make it be in your mind. Therefore it can be compared to a hologram, an illusory but real-appearing 3-D image. Each particle of a hologram contains the entire image; the whole ocean is in the drop. It's the same with consciousness, our own holographic psyche. All the parts there ever were to our psyche are there yet in potential. We may be said to have grown up, but not grown out of potential contact with any of the parts of ourselves that were ever there.

Revisit the places you roamed and played as a kid. Dream again with the timeless abandonment to the moment you knew as a kid. Pore over old pictures, telling your children about favorite times and pastimes when you were small. And if memories of your early years aren't all that palatable, design or participate more often in activities that bring out the youngster in you (kite flying is a good one).

Remember, it's never too late to have a happy childhood!

Great men and great women are always simple and childlike. They connect with nature in a humble and unassuming way, drawing upon the healing power of the natural world. There is an elemental smell of the world, which we knew as children. Whatever it is—grass or soil or dead leaves—it can be recaptured by a short time away from the haunts of men. Have you trained your nostrils away from savoring that elemental pungency by a steady diet of the odors of civilization? Don't you need to get out and smell the natural world again? Don't you yearn to leave the ceaseless sophisticated babble, to go and rediscover your own innocence and lack of guile by observing the non-self-consciousness of little wild animals?

Have you plunged your hands into the dirt, or put your bare feet into an icy stream, or climbed a tree lately? Have you thrown yourself down on your back, even out there on your own balcony or backyard, for a prolonged reacqaintance with the stars? Or stood on a snowy mountaintop on skis, sucked in the tinkling icy air while below you the forest and valley stretch away in the muted tones of winter? Or sat on a seaside rock promontory and felt your oneness with the great waves rolling in?

Walt Whitman's poem "Song of the Open Road" fittingly concludes this step:

Afoot and light-hearted I take to the open road,
Healthy, free, the world before me,
The long brown path before me leading wherever I choose.
Henceforth I ask not good-fortune, I myself am good-fortune,
Henceforth I whimper no more, postpone no more, need
    nothing,
Done with indoor complaints, libraries, querulous criticisms,
Strong and content I travel the open road.

STEP 18

Practice Gratefulness

Most of us have been given many more blessings than we have received.

—RACHEL NAOMI REMEN

A Japanese tea ceremony begins, "Appreciation with discernment is the secret gateway to the abounding life." This suggests that sincere giving of thanks for what one has opens the way to receiving more. This paradox is reflected in Western medicine as well, where it has long been assumed that an effective strategy for enhancing one's emotional life is to count one's blessings. Several studies by the National Institute of Healthcare Research suggest that the conscious practice of gratefulness has ramifications for health and well-being. One study showed that adults who kept gratitude journals on a weekly basis exercised more regularly, reported fewer physical symptoms, felt better about their lives as a whole, and were optimistic about the upcoming week compared to those who recorded hassles or neutral life events.

Gratitude works. Robert A. Emmons, a professor of psychology at the University of California at Davis, says that focusing on the gifts one has been given is an antidote to envy, resentment, regret, and other negative states that undermine long-term happiness. Gratefulness is a different way to look at things. It searches out and recognizes evidences of providential supply. With so much scarcity, fear, and uncertainty in the collective consciousness these days, there are lots of payoffs from greeting each day with a smile and saying, "Thanks for everything!"

A person, said Abraham Lincoln, is generally about as happy as he is willing to be. What if today were the best day of your life, and you didn't know it? If you didn't know it, you wouldn't act like it, so chances are, the best day of your life would pass you right by. Attitude is everything; when we fail to appreciate what we have, we miss the real blessing of it. Dramas such as the play *Our Town* and the film *It's a Wonderful Life* have tried to tune us in to the fact that, as Martin Buber reminded us, just to live is holy.

Denial of Gratefulness

In her book *My Grandfather's Blessings,* Dr. Rachel Naomi Remen quotes one of her patients who described her image of the many gifts going unappropriated by people. "We're all being circled by our blessings, sometimes for years, like airplanes in a holding pattern at an airport, stacked up with no place to land." Before we enumerate the ways we can stay on the upside of life, let's review several attitudes Remen mentions that keep people from fully recognizing the fortuitous events in their lives. See if any of these rings a bell with you.

The "Special" Argument

Perhaps I think, *Well, something has to be pretty special or outstanding for me to notice enough to give thanks for it.* But then I find that when I think to *practice* thanksgiving ("Thanks for this safe car to drive … thanks for that tree in the meadow with its branches tossing in the wind ... thanks for the good lunch I just had"), I am changed and uplifted.

As Ray Bradbury, on receiving the National Book Foundation's Medal for Distinguished Contribution to American Letters, 2000, said, "There's no use having a universe, a cosmology, if you don't have witnesses. We are the witnesses to the miracle. We are put here by creation, by God.... We're here to be the audience to the magnificent. It is our job to celebrate."

The "Troubles" Argument

What's to be thankful for, when I have to endure these troubles? One answer is suggested by the Great Barrier Reef, which stretches some eighteen hundred miles from New Guinea to Australia. Tour guides regularly take visitors to view the reef. One traveler noticed that the lagoon side of the reef looked pale and lifeless, while the ocean side was vibrant and colorful. She asked the guide about it. The guide replied, "The coral around the lagoon side is in still water, with no challenge for its survival. It dies early. The coral on the ocean side is constantly being tested by wind, waves, and storms. These surges of power cause it to fight for survival every day of its life. As it is challenged and tested, it changes and adapts. It grows healthy and strong, and it reproduces. That's the way it is with every living organism."

Rachel Naomi Remen agrees. "Sometimes," she writes, "a wound is the place where we encounter life for the first time, where we come to know its power and its ways. Wounded, we may find a wisdom that will enable us to live better than any knowledge and glimpse a view of ourselves and of life that is both true and unexpected."

The "Entitlement" Argument

Another way to blind ourselves to our blessings is to act entitled to them. *It's about time! With all the stuff I've been going through,*

I've got this coming to me. People in service occupations well know how irritating ungratefulness can be when they go beyond the call of duty to serve a customer's needs, only to have their efforts ignored. No matter how outstanding the effort, such customers' attitude says, "You're just doing your job." Waitpersons who smile as they lug heavy trays around restaurants and relay complaints to the chef have a word for the experience of going tipless; they call it being "stiffed." It perfectly describes the unbending attitude of entitlement.

Benefits of Gratefulness

Your active practice of appreciating and giving thanks on every hand opens your life to a variety of benefits, such as the following.

Guidance

Gratefulness is a way to be guided. With the keener vision of a grateful heart you will see the countless ways the Infinite Kindness is guiding you and molding you into what you can become. The heart-opening that is part of thanksgiving makes you more sensitive to the nuances in events around you that will lead you in the right way. You begin to wake up to things you ignored before, and to see them intuitively as guideposts. You register each one mentally and hold it in wonder, jumping to no conclusions but thinking delightfully, *That's fishy!*

Winks

Gratefulness opens your heart to recognize those little happystances that banish loneliness by reminding you that a Loving Power is in your corner. The more thankful you are, the more tuned in you feel to the way things work, and the more you notice a divine serendipity taking place through everyday events. Each "wink" reminds you that you are loved and protected, and causes you to be more grateful than ever. The humdrum aspects recede, and life becomes an adventure.

Friendship

The experience of gratitude and the actions stimulated by it build and strengthen social bonds and friendships. Grateful people are more fun to be around. Their generous spirit creates more space for others to be themselves. Appreciators have more fun. It's hard to get someone down who's always rejoicing about something.

Empowerment

Gratefulness is a special use of energy—it expands with use. By the simple practice of remembrance (inwardly chanting, "Thank you for this, thank you for that") you align yourself with the Cosmic Bank, the Divine Dynamo that supplies more and more energy.

Mind Like Water Exercises

■ *Whisper Thanks All Day*

Whenever you have a moment, bring more thankfulness into your mind and heart. When you see someone less fortunate, don't look away. Take it as an opportunity to give thanks for the blessings you enjoy. When you experience a setback, say thank you. It will open your eyes to the benefits that are often hidden in times of apparent calamity or disaster. It will cause you to think of yourself as a life-long learner who is in it for the long haul. When you pray, don't ask for things. Instead give thanks, and request help to see and appreciate all the love and abundance that is yours.

■ *Appreciate Nature*

If ever there was a nature appreciator, it was Henry David Thoreau. A passage from one of his journals shows the receptivity of one who sees and hears things others miss: "To make a perfect winter day like today, you must have a clear, sparkling air, with a sheen from the snow, sufficient cold, little or no wind, and the warmth must come directly from the sun. It must not be a thawing warmth. The tension of nature must not be relaxed. The earth must be resonant if bare, and you hear the lisping tinkle of chickadees from time to time, and the unrelenting steel-cold scream of a jay."

■ *Figure Everything's a Gift*

If it makes you glad, give thanks for it. If not, look for the bless in the mess—the lesson, the learning, the hidden message that causes us sometimes to look back on hard things with realization of how they graced us by causing us to grow, or learn, or change.

■ *Enlarge Your Cup*

The secret of receptivity is increased capacity. As you go on into the day, think: How could I be taking in more? Say: "There is a lot out there today. Let me not miss any of it." Use these affirmations to expand your ability to receive:

- I'm too busy being grateful for what I've been given to feel bad about what I lack.
- I am a smile millionaire.
- I always have plenty of what I need.
- I am one of the walking wealthy, rich in the things that count.
- All things work together for my good.

■ *Become a Militant Optimist*

Militant optimism is a ferocious commitment to being happy. The militant optimist (MO) adopts a positive attitude toward life in general, and about each and every moment of it in particular. The MO realizes that problems are life's way of training us to be tough. As sportswriter Charles P. Pierce wrote: "Optimism is not necessarily blind. It is neither weak nor naïve. It can be tough and pure and earned just as clearly as any brooding existential despair."

■ *Use "I Get To"*

In the morning, after your time of quiet, as you're beginning to think about the day ahead, write down (or imagine writing down) three sentences that begin with the words "I have to ..." Then, on paper or mentally, change the word "have" to the word "get" in each phrase. Thus "I have to's" become "I get to's." See how that shakes up the Etch A Sketch of your mind.

■ *Stay in the Moment*

Let go of the past. Whenever you're tempted to regret something, usher your attention back from the done-and-gone. If you spot a worry about the future, bring your mind back from that event. Give yourself, over and over again, the gift of the Present.

Open-hearted enjoyment of what one has, especially in times of adversity, shields the consciousness from fear, discouragement, sadness, and cynicism—inner enemies that kill passion and sap enthusiasm. If you train yourself to be grateful even in the midst of difficulties, you will discover a hidden blessing behind every adversity. Mental, physical, and emotional well-being are enhanced by the spirit of gratefulness. A thankful heart is a healthy heart. An active thanker maintains a strong spiritual immune system.

If thankfulness does not come naturally to you, fake it till you make it. Particularly if times are stressful, you'll need to practice gratefulness consciously and consistently, to get the flow going. But then little come-ons will show up. You'll find yourself thankful for what happened *because* you were thankful. In time you'll begin to enjoy just having the thankful attitude; it will make you happier and more fun to be around. You'll start to anticipate whatever will happen, even a challenge, because you'll know now that eventually it will bring you the gift of thankfulness. For example, next time you're caught in rush-hour gridlock, don't get mad, get grateful. Sit back, breathe deeply, and say, "Thanks. I needed a slowdown."

implacability

❧

By steady, tireless wearing away, water changes and ultimately destroys the hardest surfaces. In this work it is patient and unhurried.

Lesson: Value the step you are on in your development. Take pride in whatever task you are doing. Be patient, willing to plod. Always go for the long run.

Know Your Mission

Average people are goal-driven. Leaders are mission-driven.

—LEADERSHIP DEVELOPMENT GROUP

One day an expert in time management was speaking to a group. He pulled out a one-gallon, wide-mouthed Mason jar and set it on the table in front of him. He also produced about a dozen fist-sized rocks and carefully placed them one at a time into the jar. When the jar was filled to the top and no more rocks would fit inside, he asked, "Is this jar full?"

Everyone agreed that it was. He then reached under the table and pulled out a bucket of coarse gravel. He dumped some of the gravel in and shook the jar, causing pieces of gravel to work themselves down into the spaces between the rocks. He then asked the group once more, "Is the jar full?" This time some members of the group were not so sure. "Good!" he said as he reached under the table and brought out a bucket of sand and dumped it in the jar. Everyone watched as he shook the jar again and the sand filtered down around the gravel. Once more he

175

asked the question, "Is the jar full?" No one answered. He then grabbed a pitcher of water and kept on pouring it in until the jar was filled to the brim. He looked at the glass and asked, "What's the point of this illustration?"

One bright young man said, "The point is, no matter how full your schedule is, if you really think about it you can always fit in more things."

The time management expert shook his head. "What this illustration teaches us is this: *If you don't put the big rocks in first, you'll never get them in at all.*"

What are the big rocks in your life? Time with your loved ones? Your dreams? Your health? A worthy cause? What are the big rocks for you at work? What are the things that make the biggest difference, that can help your organization not only survive but thrive? The 80/20 rule says that 80 percent of the results you get come from 20 percent of your activity. Now more than ever it's necessary to focus on priorities. *The most important thing in life is to decide what the most important thing in life is.*

The Videotape Exercise

Plato said, "The unexamined life is not worth living." What a shame it would be to spend your life climbing a ladder, only to discover at the end that it was the wrong ladder! Times of constant change pose a paradox: greater need to know where we're going, but less time to reflect on it and make sure it's right. The pace of life today requires each of us to become a philosopher—someone who thinks about thinking, who examines life and tries to figure out what it's all about. How can we get up above the circumstances and conditions of life to figure out the answers? One way is to imagine time as a videotape.

Here is an activity you can do right now in your imagination, that will expand your consciousness. Mentally see yourself standing, looking down on a table with a VCR on it. Remove the cover of the machine and see the two reels with the tape paused at the player head in the front. One reel holds the unplayed tape—that's the future. The other, the take-up reel, is the past.

Lift the two reels out of the machine and spread the tape. Now you can see all the moments of your life at once. At one end is when you were born; at the other, when you die. The frames near the player head represent the present. Look at that section—that represents this week. Do you see yourself rushing through life? Why all the hurry? (Hopefully it isn't just to get into the ground sooner!)

Now, keeping in mind this overall perspective of having seen life, as it were, all at once, ask yourself, *What does all the activity of my days really stand for? What is my life supposed to be all about?* Once you have asked and answered the following questions about your key operating values and your overarching purpose, you can look back at the present and see if what you're doing makes sense, whether it *fits*.

Choosing Your Top Values

If it's true that the most important thing in life is to decide what is most important, what should you stand for? What ideals should govern your actions and decisions? Specifically, what should be the key values by which you operate? Look over the following list of values and circle any that "jump out" because of their importance to you. Then write your top three values in the spaces at the bottom, in the order of their importance to you. Feel free to add values if you need to.

truth	persistence	wealth	efficiency
sincerity	dependability	initiative	fun
communication	understanding	attention to detail	family

trust	environment	relationships	excellence
pride	faith	calmness	mission
power	wisdom	teamwork	control
flexibility	service	courage	perspective
profitability	competition	passion	friendship
excitement	recognition	creativity	learning
influence	happiness	honesty	justice
honor	quality	originality	innovation
candor	hard work	obedience	prosperity
responsiveness	financial security	fulfillment	respect
community	fairness	purpose	integrity
order	strength	peace	loyalty
collaboration	love	security	humor
support	adventure	cleverness	success
cooperation	endurance	bravery	nationality

My Top Three Values

1. _____
2. _____
3. _____

Composing a Personal Mission Statement

Now that your have clarified your values, you can incorporate them into a personal mission statement, an overarching expression of your purpose in life and work. Once you have completed a draft of your mission, you will be among the top 5 percent of human beings in the world in these terms. Most people are so busy coping with the exigencies of life that they don't realize they can stop and figure out where they're going. They are like Alice who, when she encountered the Cheshire cat and asked him which road to take, was asked, "Where are you going?" "I don't know," she answered. "Then any road will do," the cat replied.

Average people are goal-driven. Leaders are mission-driven. Having a mission statement automatically puts you ahead in life. It energizes you with a conscious sense of purpose, adds meaning to your activities and romance to your life. With a consciousness of mission, you can see yourself on a hero's journey.

Advantages of Writing Your Mission Statement

Even a rough first draft of your mission can save you much time by guiding your decision-making. Once your mission is formulated and written down in words, things will show up differently in your daily life. For instance, you will recognize immediately those things you can say no to, for they are not aligned with the business you've decided you are in.

You also can measure priorities against your statement. Once you have composed it, copy your statement on the front page of your planner. Review it each morning before turning to your to-do list for the day, then mark each item on that list with a 1, 2, or 3, depending on its degree of importance as measured by your mission statement. Go into the day determined to get some 3s done! That night, as you lie in bed before sleep, review the day, focusing on two or three events or accomplishments that link with your mission statement. This further implants the consciousness that you are on a mission, a journey of fulfillment.

Following is a simple two-stage plan for composing a first draft of your personal mission statement.

Stage 1: Listing

List nouns in column 1. List verbs in column 2. Write a description in column 3.

1. Some of my gifts and acquired skills:	2. Some ways I influence and contribute to others:	3. My vision of a better world:
_____ _____ _____ _____	_____ _____ _____ _____	_____ _____ _____ _____

Examples:

organization, musical ability, math	listen, teach, show kindness	more peaceful

Stage 2: Combining

Choose 2 items each from columns 1 and 2 above. Combine these with your vision of a better world.

To use my...	to...	so that...
_____ _____ _____	_____ _____ _____	_____ _____ _____

Example: *To use my* creativity and sense of humor *to* coach and provide an example for people *so that* they become more light-hearted and accepting of life's ups and downs.

You will probably want to work with your mission statement to streamline and fit it to your own style of speaking and thinking. Use evocative word pictures to visualize it in a more compelling way.

Mind Like Water Exercises

■ *Review Your Mission Every Day*

At least when you enter your day, or when you take time in your sacred space, you need to review your mission and let it *re-mind* you. How will you keep your mission in the forefront of your mind? Some obvious ways are to post it where you will see it—in the front of your planner, on your mirror, refrigerator door, or the dashboard of your car. Each morning when you are about to turn to your to-do list of tasks for the day, spend time with your mission statement, thinking of the day as a part of fulfilling it. Each night, before you go to sleep, look back over the day and identify events and actions that showed you were "on purpose" in a larger way.

■ *Edit Your Mission*

Your mission statement should not read like a duty or a burden. It should ring your emotional chimes. While it is broad and far-reaching—enough to encompass every area of your life and work—your statement should be unique and special to you. Work with it so the wording uplifts and inspires you, or dazzles others when you share it with them.

■ *Keep a Journal*

In the morning, or before going to bed, reflect on the day and write your thoughts and feelings. Analyze your experiences. Every few days or weeks, read back through your entries, recalling when you wrote each one. Notice that the thing you wanted, or wished to have happen, was accomplished—or not. Things turned out as you expected them to—or not. This review is a little like the videotape exercise, in that it gets you above the "petty pace" so you can see again that life has a way of working itself out, regardless of your worries or your tendency to "sweat the small stuff."

■ Practice Aboveness

In the midst of activity, pause and "zoom out"—go in imagination to ceiling level and look down on yourself. See your living body in the context of the room or the environment. Watch the thoughts turning in your head. For a few calm moments, in a detached manner, observe whatever's going on down there. Then zoom back.

■ Stop and Think

Whenever you can during the busy times, pause and take a breath. Ask yourself, *Is this activity of mine in alignment with my life mission?* If the answer is yes, smile. If no, pause and question. If you are in the wrong job or the wrong relationship, writing and reviewing a personal mission statement does not necessarily make the situation more pleasant, but it highlights the gap between where you are and where you want to go. Perhaps there is a way to influence things to bring them more in line with your values. Maybe confrontation is in order. Maybe other plans must be made.

Knowing "the meaning of life" has never been as important. In overbusy times it's so easy to get off course, we had better know and define clearly what on course means. In a society in which most people are just coping, having a mission statement doubtless puts you in the personal-power elite. Most folks think of a mission as some difficult task to aspire to, or as an obscure dream too difficult to figure out. Your mission was there before you wrote it down. It's the journey you've always been on. You've rediscovered it by giving it a form that combines and focuses your natural talents and strengths and preferences into a major purpose. Your mission serves you as you serve it. It helps you to say no to things that are not on your path. It makes decisions easier by defining what business you are really in. It keeps you from straying and sampling. It aligns your forces and energies in a single direction. It leads you ultimately to be satisfied and fulfilled in life.

Become a Warrior

The free mind is the fruit of an austere law: it has to be reconquered day by day. It subsists in a state of war and belongs only to those who fight for it.

—VAN WYCK BROOKS

Meeting challenges is part of life and growth. Many people can identify with the term "warrior" today, because each morning when they get up and face the day, it feels to them like they're going to war. Everyone is to some extent engaged in the battle of life. In this step, however, it is important to differentiate being a warrior from the notion of human conflict. The warrior as here defined is a person of peace—a peaceful warrior, if you will. As Tibetan Buddhist Chogyam Trungpa writes in *Shambhala, the Sacred Path of the Warrior,* "Warriorship does not refer to making war on others. Aggression is the source of our problems, not the solution."

What, then, is a warrior? There is great similarity among traditions of many times and cultures regarding warriorship. The

Shambhala teachings of Tibet resemble those of Native American tribes as well as the samurai tradition in Japan. Jewish and Christian ideals of the warrior gathered around great rulers of the Bible such as King David. Later the principles of enlightened warriorship found expression in the legends of King Arthur and others. All of these define warriorship as a tradition of human bravery.

In Eastern societies the concept of being a warrior was founded on a premise that there is basic human wisdom that can help to solve the world's problems. We will focus on bravery here as well—and enlightened courage. Being a warrior means seeking and finding that wisdom and embodying it in the way one lives and relates to the world. Another way to put this is to say that the warrior seeks enlightenment, and by his or her actions seeks to foster an enlightened society.

Overcoming Fear of Ourselves

The work of becoming a warrior must begin with oneself, for we are subject to fears of ourselves and our world. Growing up from being tiny and totally dependent, many humans tend to develop an early fear of their environment. Even in adulthood many still see the world as basically threatening. The enlightened definition of bravery is one of overcoming this basic fear or, as Trungpa declares, not being afraid of yourself. "When we are afraid of ourselves and afraid of the seeming threat the world presents," he writes, "then we become extremely selfish."

This simple statement explains much of the chaos that persists in the world, not only within families and societies but also between and among nations. It sheds light on the hoarding and self-protectiveness we see; it explains the gulf that always seems to persist between the "haves" and the "have-nots." (As Cardinal Richelieu said, "Nations do not have principles, they have preferences.") All that selfishness comes from fear. If we could but lose that fear, we would open our hearts to our own goodness and generosity.

The first task of becoming a warrior, then, is to overcome fear of ourselves. When we are frightened, we become selfish, addicted to comfort, wanting our own way all the time, and manipulated by our likes and dislikes. Overcoming our basic fear can heal us of these things. Mind Like Water always implies the simpler way, the shorter way, the enlightened way, the easier way. (Think of the meaning of that word "enlightened"; it implies not only the power of illumination but also the relief of a way that is not heavy or burdensome.) Instead of flailing away at the darkness of our ego-driven negative qualities or actions, we can bring light into our minds; when we do, the darkness is automatically dissipated. Thus an important way of losing our fear of ourselves is, to use Trungpa's phrase, by discovering our basic goodness.

Discovering Our Basic Goodness

A certain ache or ailment that has been with you a long time becomes accepted in time as normal; sometimes you don't realize you had it until it's gone. In the same way, you might not know you have a fear of yourself until you lose it; then it is conspicuous in its absence. That's the way it was when I rediscovered my own basic goodness one winter night years ago, just before the holidays when I took a walk from where I was living out toward a nearby seawall park. As I trudged through the snowpacked streets, gazing at the Christmas lights in the windows, I became aware of a subtle difference in my perceptions. Everything looked slightly altered, as if the very air I was looking through were transformed.

I stopped to ponder this, aware of a trickling of joy within me, as well. Then it came to me, the thing that was so different about the world I was looking at: it was, for the first time, *my world.* I no longer was an alien in it; I belonged in it. I had a perfect right to be in it, without apology, without explanation or justification. With this realization every sensory experience was heightened. The cold air, the distant stars, the tree lights, the sound of waves gently breaking on the beach, all poured through my senses. I had thought I was alive before, yet now suddenly I knew I had not been. This was what it was like to be really alive!

I knew I had reached a milestone that night. Through that sudden, inexplicable absence of fear and trepidation I discovered that I had been afraid before, perhaps to some degree all my life. No longer need I look over my shoulder at life; life was mine to face, and it was my friend. I was in wonder. I felt so liberated I wanted to celebrate; so I did, privately, as I continued my walk, laughing and singing and hugging myself through the cold, crisp night air.

Chogyam Trungpa teaches that as warriors we must accept responsibility for uplifting our lives. A great deal of the chaos in the world is because people don't appreciate themselves. Many take their existence for granted or find it depressing and burdensome. As human beings, Trungpa says, we have a working basis within ourselves that allows us to uplift our state of existence and to "cheer up fully." Developing tenderness toward ourselves allows us to see both our problems and our potential accurately. When you don't punish or condemn yourself, when you relax more and appreciate your body and mind, you begin to contact the fundamental notion of basic goodness in yourself. When you experience the goodness of being alive, you can respect who and what you are.

Tough and Nice

The challenge of being a warrior is to leave the cocoon of self-absorption and selfish separation and step out into the space of the world. It is to be at once brave and gentle, or as warriors are sometimes called, tough and nice. This dynamic combination of courage and kindliness that waits to be nurtured in the warrior is unbeatable. A prerequisite for its development is discovery of basic goodness.

One's basic goodness is not discovered once for all. Being a warrior means being on an endless journey in life. You must rediscover yourself and your goodness, says Trungpa, and each time you do so, things become simpler. That's because you are tuning yourself more closely to genuine reality, to the way things really are in the world, shorn of your preconceptions and expectations.

I recall another time long ago when I rediscovered myself, and how it made everything very simple. (Have you discovered that when you reach a state of self-acceptance, things seem suddenly simplified? It's not that the world is complicated; it is that our state of mind makes everything look that way.) Weeks before, I had gone through an intense process of arranging payments to the IRS on my previous year's back taxes, and assumed all was in order. Then one day I received a notice saying my payment had not been received. Its threatening note sent me into gales of self-recrimination.

I took a walk around the block to cool off. There I was, steaming along and all but taking a whip to my back, when suddenly a message dawned in my brain. I didn't actually hear a voice, but I might as well have. *You are a child of God.* I stopped, struck by the sudden silencing of all those biting voices of my inward self-critics, and the concomitant filling of my whole body-mind with ecstasy. For the rest of my trip around the block I was all but skipping!

Again, rediscovery of our basic goodness has the power to un-complicate. With the reclamation of my esteem I could suddenly see the situation in its true light. There was no problem with the IRS; I would simply go home, call the agent, and inform him of the truth—that I had mailed the payment the day before. It was fear that drove that self-punishment, and when by grace the light came in so I could clearly appreciate myself, the darkness of that fear was dispelled, and everything became clear and simple.

Chuang-tze, a contemporary of Plato, said, "If you have insight, you use your inner eye, your inner ear, to pierce to the heart of things, and have no need of intellectual knowledge." Carl G. Jung's research led him to contend that the unconscious is possessed of absolute knowledge, and that every microcosmic event is charged with macrocosmic events. Jung was very interested in chance occurrences of events apparently not connected through cause; he called the principle behind such events *synchronicity* to designate their meaningful cross-connection.

Once one takes the warrior's path, synchronicity plays a larger part than before. In a random-and-meaningless-appearing world, it is useful to consciously connect one's life journey to the idea of an unfolding story. As a warrior, you are playing a role in this larger story; as in any well-told tale, events are connected, but it's not always clear just how. The notion that you are playing a role in a story causes you to notice things in a new way. You are looking for those clues and connections, for the divine infrastructure that lies just behind appearances. As you begin to recognize in everyday events the hand of a Cosmic Storyteller, everyday happenings take on a romantic glow. People, objects, and events you would not have noticed before now seem imbued with fresh meaning. You open your heart in wonder. You do not "know" things you knew before, but you are having more fun. Once you have, not a passing belief but an absolute conviction that nothing happens by accident, life becomes an exciting adventure. *Everything means it.*

All for Our Good

The world of animal training knows much about command-and-control tactics. Many dog-owners use fear and punishment to induce obedience. But there is another way to get not only the behavior you want from an animal but also its love. My friends Thad Lacinek and Chuck Tompkins, have the fascinating job of training the killer whales that perform in the Shamu Show at Sea World. Chuck told me, "There is one key idea we seek to convey to the animals from the first day we start to work with them: *We mean you no harm.* You can trust us. We would not think of abusing or misusing you, or causing you any fear or sense of punishment or deprivation."

The same understanding applies, of course, to human relationships. Ken Blanchard has been my coach for many years. In his books and through his many speeches and keynote addresses, Ken is continually telling top business executives, managers, coaches, teachers, and parents to "catch people doing things right." In other words, begin looking for what people do well, and when you see it, call it to their attention. Everyone wins by this method—and the good performance is strengthened.

If this positive, supportive outreach works consistently with animals and with people, must it not be the spiritual basis of our relationship with the Creator? So many people's idea of what they call God is an angry punisher, but that is not how we act toward our own children when we are at our best. By trusting that the universe means us no harm, we open ourselves to the goodness in everything around us. This eases the way for us as warriors, for when we see the neglected beauty of the world, we fall in love with it. If you are of an actively spiritual nature, you may eliminate the negative suggestion in the second assumption—the universe means us no harm—to read: *The One behind it all means everything for my good.*

Mind Like Water Exercises

■ *Overcome Fear of Yourself*
Fear of yourself leads to selfishness. As a way in to the fear, analyze your behavior. Ask: Am I constantly self-absorbed? Do I hoard things? Do I insist on my own way? Overcome self-involvement by consciously giving others credit and by trying to put them first. Remember that your upstream swim against the ego habit requires courage. You are engaging in the warrior role as you strive toward enlightened action.

■ *Seek Your Basic Goodness*
At the first hint of self-blame when you make an error, focus on the action you don't want to repeat, and away from yourself as a

perpetrator. Acknowledge your full right to a place in the universe. Remind yourself that nothing is too good for a child of God.

■ Catch Yourself Doing Things Right

Acknowledge every right action. Especially if you tend to sell yourself short, start giving yourself credit in small ways. *Nice going. That was good. I did that well.*

■ Let Yourself off the Hook

Stop berating yourself, beating yourself up for little things. Realize that you can forgive *all* past actions done to date, and do it. You don't have to carry a burden of blame, guilt, or shame. A good prayer to say: *Naughty or good, I am Thy child.*

■ Watch for Winks

Be on the lookout for serendipitous occurrences. Where one occurs, smile and acknowledge its message: The One behind it all is winking at you.

■ Catch People Doing Things Right

Start focusing on what people do right, and tell them about it. If they are learning a new skill, catch them doing it *approximately* right. Redirect attention from what they do wrong by repeating instructions and resetting the goal.

Adding Light to the World

Once you undertake the warrior's journey by rediscovering yourself and your basic goodness, you can see right action as it needs doing. Ultimately the warrior's job is to help the world be better. The warrior's way of doing this is by providing an enlightened example for others to follow. As someone has said, "Do you want world peace? Make peace in your own life. Do you want kindness and unselfishness to increase in the world? Be kind and unselfish yourself."

Often this means doing the thing that no one else is doing. Sometimes that action is not popular; sometimes it makes no sense to others. But once you have discovered your basic goodness and learned to trust it, you can listen to your heart to tell you the right thing to do. As a warrior, you can learn how to be in the world without any deception, to be fully genuine and alive. By being open and honest with yourself, you can learn to be open and honest with others. On the basis of the goodness you discover in yourself, you can connect with the goodness in others.

The warrior assumes basic goodness in others even if it is well hidden. He or she has faith that acting on the basis of universal basic goodness is the right way regardless of the other person's attitude or response. He or she does not wait for evidence of goodness in others to treat them that way but acts *anyway*.

The so-called Paradoxical Commandments of Leadership capture this sense of indomitable goodwill. Originally composed in 1968 by Kent Keith while a student at Harvard College, these guidelines have found their way into a great many speeches and publications. Mother Teresa kept a version of them pinned on her wall.

Paradoxical Commandments of Leadership

1. People are illogical, unreasonable, and self-centered. *Love them anyway.*
2. If you do good, people will accuse you of selfish ulterior motives. *Do good anyway.*
3. If you are successful, you win false friends and true enemies. *Succeed anyway.*
4. The good you do today will be forgotten tomorrow. *Do good anyway.*
5. Honesty and frankness make you vulnerable. *Be honest and frank anyway.*

6. The biggest people with the biggest ideas can be shot down by the smallest people with the smallest minds. *Think big anyway.*

7. People favor underdogs but follow only top dogs. *Fight for a few underdogs anyway.*

8. What you spend years building may be destroyed overnight. *Build anyway.*

9. People really need help, but may attack you if you do help them. *Help them anyway.*

10. Give the world the best you have and you'll get kicked in the teeth. *Give the world the best you have anyway.*

Be an Everyday Hero

The credit belongs to the man who is actually in the arena ... who strives valiantly, who knows the great enthusiasms, the great devotions, and spends himself in worthy causes. Who, at best, knows the triumph of high achievement and who, at worse, if he fails, fails while daring greatly, so that his place shall never be with those cold and timid souls who know neither victory nor defeat.

—THEODORE ROOSEVELT

Self-change is the mark of real courage. There is a rule in fiction writing that says "The hero is the one who changes." True heroism, the everyday variety, is going upstream against yourself, answering to what you know you should do rather than to your own fears and addictions. The problem human beings face during difficult times is the choice between retreating to the comfort zone, or advancing without prospect of reward. By choosing the latter, we awaken the hero and dispel sorrow.

The great teacher and mythologist Joseph Campbell recognized that the world's great myths contain clues to universal truths that can be applied to the human and cosmic mysteries that every person must in time confront. By the time of his death in 1987 his main interest had become that of synthesizing the mythical themes of many times and places. Struck by their remarkable similarities, he became convinced that "there is only one myth."

Campbell's advice to students was: "Follow your bliss." Although he taught no particular brand of ideology or theology, his research had a definite spiritual dimension. Campbell felt that myths help people to recognize the Transcendent in their personal worlds, and thus fulfill the human need for experiencing the divine presence. The tale of the hero's journey particularly captivated Campbell, and became the subject of his book *The Hero with a Thousand Faces*.

The basic motif for the hero's journey, Campbell said, is "leaving one condition of life and finding the source of life to bring you forth in a richer or more mature condition." (A better statement of intention for the present book could not be found.) He took this myth to be the model for the adventure that each of us must undertake as he or she journeys through the uncertainties of life. The Hero's Journey consists of several stages.

Stage One: Leaving Home

Campbell explained that while in many heroic tales the main character sets off with the conscious intention of performing a deed, in the more common motif the hero simply finds himself or herself suddenly swept up in an adventure. This is the situation of the person in modern life: with all the changes happening, we appear to have been thrown into a maelstrom. Most of us experience relocations in these fast-paced, restless times, so we are familiar with the concept of leaving home. But leaving home can mean much more than forsaking one place of residence or employment for another.

Psychologically speaking, leaving home means moving out of our comfort zone—those accustomed habits and routines of thinking and behaving on which we have come to rely but that do not reflect our commitment to a life of deeper values. A person may step onto the hero's path reluctantly, like John Wayne in the Western adventure movie *Big Jake.* Wayne plays Jake, a wandering loner trying to stay out of trouble when he comes across some cattlemen about to hang an innocent sheepherder. Just as Jake is resolving to go on his way and not get involved, the victim's young son rushes up, trying to prevent the hanging, and is brutally kicked aside by one of the assailants. "Now what," says Jake with a sigh, "did they have to go and do *that* for?" Regretfully, he rides into the scene, drawn onto the path of the hero by his own standard of integrity.

This is like the call to the hero's journey for most of us. Unlike most of the classic heroes who went on a stated mission of valor, our condition appears to be one of: *We did not intend it, but here we are in it. Now what?* The comfort-loving ego demands that we hide out from the storm, seek refuge in some cave of habit or ease, just until the weather lets up. But the truth is that change is not going to let up.

Stage Two: Overcoming Great Odds

The greatest act of heroism always has been overcoming personal attachments and weaknesses. Most often in the adventure myths and tales of the past, the hero must conquer his or her fear of the unknown, or of an enemy or other danger that lurks in his path. Frequently in the classic myths the hero encounters an opposing force that is outwardly much stronger or even seemingly invincible, such as a Goliath or a dragon. In this case, the hero must devise a way to win by his wits.

Campbell's studies showed that the awesome dragon that blocks the warrior's way is indeed invincible, that no mere knowledge or experience can overcome it. What is needed is a trick, a technique that has a secret power that will work when all else fails.

In many versions of the myth this takes the form of a magic talisman or a special teaching given by a mentor.

The most potent magic potion available to us today for overcoming the evil enemies that lurk within us as fears, prejudices, habits, and addictions is a commitment to reinvent ourselves. Today, even in business, people are accepting the fact that they must look within and reconfigure their old ideas about what life is all about. Steven Covey, in his best-selling book *The Seven Habits of Highly Effective People,* describes a set of strategies that are based on a commitment to personal integrity and moral action—heroic qualities applied to making a living. Leaders learn to write mission statements, commit them to memory, post them in their offices, and align their management practices with their principles. Says John Kotter, a professor at Harvard Business School, "Learning is directly related to people's capacity to success these days. You grab a challenge, act on it, then honestly reflect on why your actions worked or didn't. You learn from it and move on. That continuous process of lifelong learning helps enormously in a rapidly changing economic environment."

Many times the "overcoming" of the everyday hero means doing the best with what you've got. No use wishing we had been dealt a stronger hand. Rebellion against our handicaps doesn't help, nor does self-pity or blaming a chaotic, unpredictable environment. In the end one is left to accept oneself as a bundle of possibilities and join the world's most interesting game—that of marshaling one's own greatness out of one's own native resources. The following poem by Edward Sill grandly illustrates this principle:

> This I beheld, or dreamed it in a dream:
> There spread a cloud of dust along a plain;
> And underneath the cloud, or in it, raged
> A furious battle, and men yelled, and swords
> Shocked upon swords and shields. A prince's banner
> Wavered, then staggered backward, hemmed by foes.

A craven hung along the battle's edge,
And thought, "Had I a sword of keener steel—
That blue blade that the king's son bears—but this
Blunt thing—!" he snapped and flung it from his hand,
And lowering crept away and left the field.
Then came the king's son, wounded, sore bestead,
And weaponless, and saw the broken sword,
Hilt-buried in the dry and sodden sand,
And ran and snatched it, and with battle shout
Lifted afresh he hewed his enemy down,
And saved a great cause that heroic day.

Stage Three: Persisting

"A saint is a sinner who never gave up." The quality that most often distinguishes the hero is not courage but persistence. Thomas Huxley wrote, "Perhaps the most valuable result of all education is the ability to make yourself do the thing you have to do, when it ought to be done, whether you like it or not. It is the first lesson that ought to be learned." Genius, some have said, is only the power of making continuous efforts. Life is a little like mining: You don't sit back and wait for the hole to dig itself. You work ahead continually, not knowing if or when you'll strike pay dirt, but trusting to be led to the strike.

Keeping on keeping on is the mark of one who overcomes. In his wonderful little book *Mastery,* George Leonard writes of the process of mastering anything truly worthwhile. He advises the aspiring adept to make a commitment that will last over the long haul and "enjoy the inevitable spurts of progress and the fruits of accomplishment, then serenely accept the new plateau that waits just beyond—until the summit of accomplishment is ultimately attained."

The hero of the classic myth always had a mission to accomplish. It was this mission that inspired the hero and enabled him or her to keep going despite troubles and setbacks. Sometimes the person didn't know what the mission was until he or she was well on the way. There are great advantages to developing and maintaining awareness of the mission you are on, as against being ignorant of it. (Step 19, "Know Your Mission," is all about this.) Now as ever, the most important thing in life is to decide what the most important thing is. Without an overarching purpose in life, handling unceasing change can be like wandering in a dark, bewildering forest.

"Prospects may seem darkest when really they're on the turn," wrote Elbert Hubbard. "A little more persistence, a little more effort, and what seemed hopeless failure may turn to glorious success. There is no failure except in no longer trying." Ray A. Kroc, founder of McDonald's, states that he is convinced that to be a success in business "you must be first, you must be daring, and you must be different." He has embodied these ideas into a now-famous motto "Press On." He says,

> Nothing in the world can take the place of persistence. Talent will not; nothing is more common than unsuccessful men with talent. Genius will not; unrewarded genius is almost a proverb. Education alone will not; the world is full of educated derelicts. Persistence and determination alone are omnipotent.

Stage Four: Returning

The final phase of the hero myth—returning—refers to the changed state in which the hero emerges from the journey, yet the cycle repeats. Each adventure seasons the hero a little more, fitting him or her for the next battle. When one knows that the only way out is through, it is actually possible to relish the challenge of the unexpected, in the same way that a kayaker tackles tougher and tougher rivers to prove his or her skill in the rapids.

Mind Like Water Exercises

Hero's Journey, Stage One

■ *Identify Your CZs*

A comfort zone (CZ) is by definition an area of life in which we can move around with ease and predictability. It is made up of habits, routines, relationships, objects, and places that are familiar to us. It is a good thing to have; our routines serve us in that we need not reinvent the wheel every day to get along. Hidden in every life, however, are various pockets of mediocrity. If you don't know what they are, you don't challenge them and they continue to run you and deplete your energy away from your life mission. Outside the CZ lies not only adventure but also great energy, life force, self-expression, and the thrill of victory over the ego. How do you know a comfort zone? By the feelings you experience when you start to leave it, or even get close to the edge of it—anxiety, discomfort, embarrassment, irritation, fear, etc.

■ *Identify Your CZ Project*

To have maximum payoff from the following exercises, you need to identify an area of your life or work in which you want to grow and improve. Any area will do—health, money, relationships, work, family, spiritual life, etc. Know that whatever progress you make in growing yourself in this area will benefit you in all other areas. Additionally, by working this comfort zone project you will become aware of other areas needing attention, and develop a systematic way to confront them.

Copy the following diagram onto a piece of paper or into your journal.

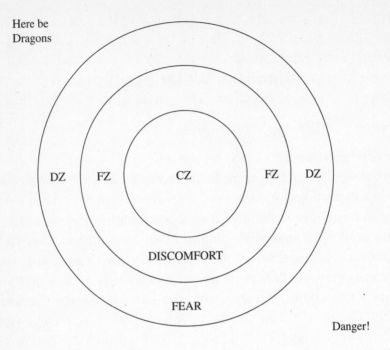

This diagram represents your comfort zone and the opportunities that lie outside it. You can use it to situate yourself, plot changes, and make experiments. In the center (CZ for Comfort Zone) place several of your favorite pastimes, places, or ideas. Scatter them about to show that this is where you feel most at home.

■ *Identify the Dangers in Leaving a CZ*

The ring just outside this is labeled FZ, for fear zone. Note that when in thought or action or by accident you cross the line, there is discomfort. Outside that line you feel anxious, unsure of yourself, like a fish out of water. You want to hurry back inside the CZ. If you are making a planned attempt to venture out, expect the temptation to be strong to go no farther.

By crossing the second line and leaving the FZ, you have entered the DZ or danger zone. This feels really scary. The feeling may not be terror; it may be shame, or intense vulnerability, a feeling of being truly at risk. You may think, "I can't stand this!" without knowing why. You want to run back to the womb of your CZ. It takes real courage to stay, for as ancient maps used to say of unexplored areas, "Here be dragons." Outside the outer circle, write down exactly what those lurking dangers might be.

■ *Identify the Payoffs for Leaving a CZ*

The Chinese symbol for crisis is made up of two characters; one is danger; the other, opportunity. In the old stories, the dragon's lair was fraught with peril, but it held a treasure. Outside the outer ring on your diagram note down some payoffs there could be for you in leaving your couch-potato CZ. (Examples: Self-esteem. Spiritual achievement. A new job. A chance to grow and learn. A spouse's pride in you. Self-evolution.)

Hero's Journey, Stage Two

■ *Identify Your Great Odds*

Should you start out on this hero's journey of self-change, know that there will be forces working for you and forces working against you. Make a list of each kind of force. For each hindering or opposing force, write down how you will or might overcome it. Make a battle plan, so that when you enter the Dark Forest and undergo an attack you will have weapons and resources at your disposal. Include material things, but also such items as the support of a friend, affirmations to repeat, visualizing success, or a way you will reward yourself on finishing the journey.

■ *Keep a Sacred Space*

How can we remain focused on what is most important while coping with life's changes and challenges? How can we keep from getting thrown off track in pursuit of lesser goals? Joseph Campbell suggested that each person find what he called a "sacred space"—a place where "you don't know what is in the news-papers, you don't know who your friends are, or who you owe money to." After a while, he believed, this solitude will become indispensable as a means of recalling "what it was that you intended."

Everyone on a hero's journey needs a place to retreat to. There the spirit is refreshed, inner strength renewed. Without those moments of letting it all go and seeking your core of values and resolution, you tend to forget what you are here for. Step 7, "Enter Your Day," is about having sacred space; whether you re-treat first thing in the morning or late at night, you need to seek solitude at least once a day. As Yogananda wrote, "As long as the conqueror in man is awake, no sorrow can cast its shadow over the threshold of his heart.... Awaken the victor in yourself, arouse the sleeping hero in yourself, and lo! No sorrow will ever again overwhelm you."

Hero's Journey, Stage Three

■ Identify Your Persisting Forces

What will you do when the going gets really tough and you are tempted to quit? Will you pray? Call a friend? Write in a diary? Play rousing music? Seek counseling? Ask yourself what you can do ahead of time to help ensure your persisting. List strategies and resources you can marshal for the rough times ahead.

■ Perform Small, Heroic Deeds

Acts of heroism usually are performed in private, without notice or fanfare. To be an everyday hero, you need not undertake a long-term task or a series of great exploits. Look for little ways to be brave every day. Is it in speaking out about something? Is it in helping someone whom everyone else has passed by? Is it quitting a habit or an addiction? Is it curbing your temper or your tendency to want things your way?

Each one of us is called upon to be an everyday hero. Life—a daily battle of joy and at the same time a passing dream—is all about growing and changing for the better, and that requires effort and fortitude. The forces that invite us to be weak and complacent or bitter and cynical are all around us. But so are other heroes, if only we look at people that way. Joseph Campbell said that each person must undertake the hero's journey on his or her own terms. But he added these reassuring words: "We have not even to risk the adventure alone, for the heroes of all time have gone before us. The labyrinth is thoroughly known. We have only to follow the thread of the hero path."

> This is the true joy in life, the being used for a purpose recognized by yourself as a mighty one; the being thoroughly worn out before you are thrown on the scrap-heap; the being a force of Nature, instead of a feverish, selfish little clod of ailments and grievances complaining that the world will not devote itself to making you happy.
>
> —GEORGE BERNARD SHAW, *Man and Superman*

essence

Though its form is ever-changing—whether appearing as ice or vapor, whether serenely placid or lashed by storm waves—water is constitutionally ever the same, itself.

Lesson: No matter what comes, no matter how you feel, keep your integrity pure. Be yourself.

Right Yourself

Our deepest fear is not that we are inadequate. Our deepest fear is that
we are powerful beyond measure. It is our light, not our darkness, that
most frightens us.

—NELSON MANDELA, 1994 inaugural speech

There's an old story about a prince who becomes bored one day
and decides to see what life outside the castle is like. He dis-
guises himself as a peasant, goes down into town, and hangs out
in a bar, where he gets drunk and passes out. He comes to in an
alley sick, dirty, and totally disoriented. He's soon swept up with
the city's horde of beggars, eating out of garbage cans and beg-
ging for pennies.

One day one of his nobleman friends finds him. He takes him
back to the castle, cleans him up, and puts him to bed. When the
prince wakes up and looks around, he recognizes his room and his
clothes. With a sigh of relief he knows he's home, where he belongs. His time of being a beggar seems only a bad dream.

Each of us is like the prince in that story. We struggle with
our cases of mistaken identity. We think we know who we are—
defining ourselves by our age, gender, race, background, body,
possessions, etc. We came from unconditional love, but were

born with amnesia and have forgotten where we came from. Again and again we must find ways to wake ourselves to our true nature, to get ourselves back to home base.

The gift of free will, with which we were also born, is a mixed blessing. Each new day we can choose the way we will go in influencing others. We can think and act in ways that empower and uplift others, or we can serve our own petty needs and hold others back. It's only when we realize that we have all the love we need that we can quit pushing and shoving our way in life. Like the prince, we need a way to awaken ourselves each new day "in our own room." We need reminders of who we really are and where we came from. This book offers reminiscences of that unconditional love from which we came, and to which we can return each new day.

To "right" something means to restore it to proper balance. A sailboat rights itself, the mast and sails standing straight up and down, after being heeled over on their side by the wind. "Righting" is a good term to use to describe mental-emotional-spiritual poise. Many of us have been "heeled over" so long by the gales of a fast-paced life that we've forgotten what straight up and down feels like. As the pace of life picks up, we need more ways to "right ourselves." Self-righting, or making ourselves right, has nothing to do with the ego or the mind's habitual insistence on "being right." In fact, humbleness is a mark of the self-righted. Humility comes automatically when we realize that we are not in charge, when it dawns on us that we are not the real doers of what gets done. The following exercise is a way to demonstrate this.

Each of us might be said to have an inner compass. Your task, in terms of this step, is to continuously recalibrate your mind and will to True North. Especially when you are tempted, or when the environment is chaotic and confusing, the ability to go to that compass and align yourself rightly with North will prove to be your salvation from much fear and many problems.

Thoreau wrote in *Walden* that he did not read newspapers, because, as he said, "I have read once before about a cow being hit by a train." He knew that most so-called "news" was merely recycled troubles and tragedies. The worst thing for mass media, of course, is to be ignored. I don't read daily newspapers or watch much network news on TV. Why take in sensational-ized details to which ratings-driven media give importance? TV networks are in a ratings race; each is hungry for the most inter-esting (translation: disturbing or even salacious) items to air. But does any of it really count? The avid newsreader says, "I must keep up with things." But how many of today's news items would be included in a historian's summary of important world happenings this week?

Our country has the media it deserves. If we could control the collective ego's voracious appetite for what's-hot-and-what's-not, we would spawn a more responsible reporting system. In-stead of focusing on the sensational, it would present everyday stories that uplift and inspire. Perhaps good and easy times pro-duce negative news stories, and only bad times give rise to the positive. In the weeks following the September 11 attacks the news items issuing from "ground zero," where the Twin Towers had stood, seemed to bear out this irony. Those days of tragedy and heroism made Americans reflect, "What were we so inter-ested in before?"

Our Real Enemies

Our real enemies—those who have it in for us, are antithetical to our growth and development and realization of our potential as di-vine beings, whose spies and infiltrators we should be on watch and guard against continuously—are not "out there," outside our skins. They are *in here,* inside our skins. They are the way we see things. They are three: mediocrity, conformity, and vulgarity.

Mediocrity

There's so much of this around that we miss it. It's so *there,* it's not there for us. The media's job is to sell us a bill of goods about stuff—that it's hot, that it's hip, that we *need* it. Eventually we become inured to hype, sound bytes, slam-dunk materialistic hokum, and think it's real. We get interested—What's the latest? Gotta have it!—then sucked in, till we're suffering fools within, doing what we're told without a thought. In the information age, it's the rush to keep up. The question we never sit down and ask is, "Why?"

The mediocrity enemy works to convince us of a low level of "good enough," to sign off on sham and fluff and half-done work. It tries to get us to think of the "old" values (excellence, honesty, personal integrity, simplicity, pride in work, plain living, and high thinking) as passé, dated, out of style. This enemy blinds our eyes to the truth about ourselves, convinces us that it's fine to settle for less than best.

Conformity

This guy's been working on us all our lives, but particularly went to war on us in our teen years. Its major weapon is fear of embarrassment: *Don't be different. Don't stick out. Don't seem this way or appear to be that way.* In other words, Don't be yourself.

Enemy no. 2 can be banished by risk-taking, by jumping in. By asking, not "What will people think?" but "What do *I* think?" It's dancing without worrying about who is watching. (The truth is, nobody's watching; they're all concerned about who's watching *them.*) Mandela picks this up in his address, in words following those quoted above:

We ask ourselves, "Who am I to be brilliant, gorgeous, talented and fabulous?" Actually, who are you not to be? You are a child of God. Your playing small doesn't serve the world.

There is nothing enlightened about shrinking so that other people won't feel insecure around you.

Vulgarity

It was refreshing for me to come across a quote recently by cartoonist Chris Ware, who draws the comic strip *Jimmy Corrigan: The Smartest Kid on Earth*. Ware said, "There is this arrogant sexuality to the modern world that I find very annoying. Everything has to be cool. Everything has to be sexy and fast-paced and rock-and-roll."

These straightforward words from a young man speaking of his times were for me a clarion call back to my own neglected values. They warned me of the extent to which I'd let my own perceptions of the world slip and sag. Somehow I'd forgotten that it's easy in this world to look at celebrities being crass, nasty, and egomaniacal—all those qualities that are "in" right now—and think they set a standard for the rest of us. And that what's difficult is to be self-respecting, to be true, to be clean, to be good.

Be on the lookout for these three enemies (remember, they all end with i-t-y). Not one of them is interested in your well-being. Not one of them wishes you well. Post sentries at the gates of your mind against these characters. And when you get one in your sights, shoot to kill.

Mind Like Water Exercises

■ *Listen to the Body*

Sit still for a few moments and think about all the finely tuned involuntary systems of your body that are at work. The heart is pumping, nourishing blood circulating; all the little cells lapping up nutrients; lungs exchanging carbon dioxide for oxygen; digestion breaking down substances, sending them where they are needed; muscles moving your eyes over the page as you read this; brain neurons firing; etc. The thing to see is that you are not lifting a finger to help. All this wondrous activity is proceeding with perfect order, efficiency, and timing, without your conscious awareness, much less your instigation.

If you do this exercise thoughtfully, an important realization should begin to dawn: *I am not the doer of my life. I am the consciousness through which my life is doing itself.* Once we bring our minds to this radical conclusion, it's proper to ask: Who is it, then, who is always clamoring for credit, taking over ownership, boasting, "I do this all myself!"? Answer: The ego, the little self. Whenever we see things through the medium of this boasting pretender, we not only lose sight of the liberating truth that we are not the doers, we also get in the way of the orderly procedure of daily life. We stop listening to our Selves.

■ Practice on Autopilot

Our everyday assumption of ownership for the work getting done through us exhausts us and robs us of our birthright of relaxation and enjoyment in work. Attached to end results, we connive and clamor for what is "ours," and end up selling all the moments away. What we need is a practice, a strategy for getting our egos out of the way and cooperating with the Force that is doing us. (Call it the Force, God, your Higher Power, Allah, Buddha, Life, or just Bob. It's the same.)

This thinking of activities as being performed not *by me* but *through me* may require some reframing. Scandalized, the strutting ego protests, "Hold on! This idea of some life force performing the involuntary processes of the physique is fine, but when it comes to outward tasks, *I rule!*"

Disregard that bogus protester's claims and welcome the coming again of poise and equanimity to your experience when you willingly surrender to the idea that you are not using energy—energy is using *you*. Start relishing the feeling of relaxation and composure, the absence of need or worry, the momentary detachment from outcome when you go on automatic pilot.

At different times of the day, experiment with this mind flip from *doer* to *done through.* Find out how the sense of being a channel for work energy, far from making you a nonparticipant, helps you get more done ... in less time ... with less effort!

■ Practice at Work

Each new day, tune into other systems—digestive, nervous, circulatory, glandular, etc. Pause in your activity for a moment and consciously align yourself with the silent stream of involuntary activity going on within you. Then transfer that effortlessness to your outward tasks. Experience the exhilaration of standing aside and cooperating, feeling yourself as a channel of performance energy.

Notice how refreshed and invigorated you feel at the end of a workday when things seemed to be easily performed through your instrumentality. Take this feeling home with you, continuing to play your role as a pipeline of positive energy. Rather than controlling conversations, play your part in them as mutually winning exchanges orchestrated by a hidden conductor.

■ Take No Credit

Righting ourselves restores harmony and order to life. Taking no credit for what happens is aligning ourselves with the way things really are. If we truly know and practice the idea that we're being "acted through," it's much easier to accept and forgive the things we do wrong. The I-am-not-the-doer mantra will likely be resisted, because self-blame, like self-praise, comes from the ego, and the mantra is ego-subverting. But persist. Knowing ourselves as not the doers, and acting like it, make life poetic.

■ Deal Creatively with Mistakes

One way to right yourself is to learn to value your mistakes. When you become obsessed with competing, making errors puts you at risk. Yet only when you make mistakes do you really begin to no-tice what needs attention.

Ben Zander, conductor of the Boston Philharmonic Orchestra, writes about two activities he uses with his graduate music stu-dents to help them get beyond their fear of making mistakes. In *The Art of Possibility,* a wonderful book Ben coauthored with his wife, Rosamund, he tells about teaching his students that when they make a mistake, they are to lift their arms in the air, smile, and say, "How fascinating!" He recommends that everyone try this, not only with mistakes but with all experiences we ordinarily define as "negative." The outrageous spirit of it is like going up to someone you've been afraid of, getting right in his or her face, and saying, "Boo!"

The "fascinating" strategy also reminds me of another friend's tactic. Tom Crum, a gifted martial arts teacher, wrote *The Joy of Conflict.* Each winter Tom invites people who attend his work-shops to join him on the ski slopes to learn skiing in a new way. As he works with people who have never been on skis before, he instructs them that whenever they are headed downhill and feel that a fall is inevitable, they are to yell, "YESSSSSS!" as loud as they can. Participants say it turns panic into fun; instead of tight-ening up, they transform each crash into a graceful celebration.

■ *Get an A*

The strategy of Ben Zander's I most admire is designed to get stu-dents beyond their concentration on grades, which he says are used only to compare one student with another, rather than with his or her own potential greatness. At the beginning of each class he announces that each student will get an A for the course, but they must fulfill one requirement for that grade. During the next two weeks, each person is to write Ben a letter dated the following May, beginning with the words, "Dear Mr. Zander, I got my A be-cause ..." They are to then tell in detail what will have happened in the interim that makes them deserving of this outstanding grade. They are to share not only what they accomplished as musicians but also how they developed as people.

I urge you to do the same. Take paper and pen, and date a letter one year from now. Place yourself in the future, looking back, and write a letter as if you are reporting on all the insights you have acquired and the milestones you attained during the year, as if these accomplishments were already in the past.

> If you don't toot your own horn once in a while, somebody is liable to use it for a spittoon.
>
> —KEN BLANCHARD

■ *Brighten Your Corner*

How can we make this world a better place every day? An old song had the answer: "Brighten the corner where you are." We can dispel darkness by adding light when we stop trying to change others and start purifying ourselves. Here is a short list of suggestions:

- Stop using profanity.
- Walk a mile briskly.
- Eat more fresh fruits and vegetables.
- Apologize to somebody.
- Pray. Give thanks and ask for help.
- Sunbathe.
- Read something uplifting.
- Clean out a messy drawer.
- Don't watch the news.
- Keep good company.
- Dump your stash.
- Hug somebody.
- Smile when it's hard to.
- Close your eyes and sit quietly.
- Appreciate nature.
- Be forgiven. Just don't do it again.

- Comfort a child.
- Use sweet words.
- Take the long way home.

■ *Affirm Yourself*

My friend Ken Blanchard, coauthor of *The One-Minute Manager,* often points out a pair of workplace truisms to his management audiences:

- People who feel good about themselves do better work.
- People who do better work feel good about themselves.

The interaction of these two events means that managers (teachers, coaches, parents, and corporate leaders) can induce an upward positive spiral in their relationships. By influencing either end of the equation—productivity or satisfaction—leaders affect both.

Thoreau wrote, "One can make a day of any size, and regulate the rising and setting of his own sun and the brightness of its shining." We add energy and quality to our own work by righting ourselves. Acknowledging our own basic goodness, raising our self-esteem, catching ourselves doing things right, uplifting ourselves, giving ourselves an A—all are ways to work better and happier. The ripples from our being happy, contented, and confident spread out and impact all of our relationships. Being esteemed automatically creates an esteeming world.

> I will consciously receive the light of the omnipresent Father constantly passing through me.
>
> —Paramahansa Yogananda

Seek Answers from the Heart

I have always known that at last I would take this road,
But yesterday I did not know that it would be today.

—NARIHARA

An ancient legend tells of an Eastern monarch who, plagued by worries and harassed on every side, called his wise men together. He asked them to invent a motto that would help him in time of trial or distress. It must be brief enough to be inscribed on a ring, he said, so he could have it always before his eyes. It must be appropriate to every situation, as useful in prosperity as in adversity. The wise men thought and thought, and finally came to the monarch with their magic words: *This, too, shall pass.*

Life teaches us that it knows better plans than we can imagine. In the end the best we can do is try to submerge our own desires into a calm willingness to accept what comes and to make the most of it, then wait again. When disorder rules, sometimes the wisest course is to let it.

The term "dark night of the soul" was coined by St. John of the Cross to describe a part of life's journey in which we have lost our bearings and are reduced to despair. When we read the lives of most great people, we find that disorientation and disorder happened to them. We also see that they faced up to these challenges. Eleanor Roosevelt's words both comfort and advise: "You gain strength, courage, and confidence by every experience in which you really stop to look fear in the face.... You must do the thing you think you cannot do."

The Role of Disorder

In her book *Life's Companion: Journal Writing as a Spiritual Quest,* Julia Cameron teaches that despair is the human psyche's initial reaction to disorder—a breakdown in communication with the world. "We have expected certain things to be true and they no longer appear to be true. The business fails. We're fired. Our relationship or marriage crumbles. A child falls in with drugs despite all we can do. We or our loved ones are struck with injury or illness. The state of the world or its disasters gets to us, and we feel helpless to intercede. All these concerns seem to want to destroy our already fragile sense of balance. But as soon as we decide that we are enough for them, that we can and will find our way, we have taken an important first step toward righting the boat."

When things don't go right, a usually quiet background battle within each of us intensifies. It is the battle between the personality's wish to have power *over* experience, to control all events and consequences, and the soul's wish to have power through experience, no matter what that may be. Wiser heads counsel that when something intervenes to destroy the relative order and predictability of our careful lives, we sometimes need to let it.

Dealing Creatively with Loss

Naomi Remen writes, "Every great loss demands that we choose life again. We need to grieve in order to do this. The pain we have not grieved over will always stand between us and life." These words are understandable when applied to a great loss, but what about little losses? Might not the sheer number of give-ups we experience in all the daily changes we go though add up to a state of unacknowledged grief? As we rush to handle the multiplicity of changes that face us, often unexpectedly, every day, it's easy to forget that every change we go through involves a give-up and a take-up. Change involves loss; when we deal creatively with it, it loses its power to hold us back.

I've had many seminar groups do the following writing activity. They generally find a good many *ahas* through doing it.

The Change-Grief Activity

List Changes

Take pencil and paper, and in three minutes list as many changes in your life as you can. List work changes, home changes, habit changes, body changes—all the changes you can think of. (Since change is continuous, include changes you've just gone through, changes you are facing now, and changes you anticipate.)

Note Losses

Go over the list of changes. Next to each item, write down the loss—what you had to give up when that change occurred/occurs. A "loss" is something you wish you could keep, something you miss, something you're forced to do without at cost. It may be tangible (space, equipment, money, etc.) or intangible (time, familiarity, relationships, feedback, respect, etc.) *Note:* You probably will not mark every item.

Know the Stages of Grief

- Stage 1: Denial
  You're in shock, coping outwardly with the altered situation, not yet in touch with your actual feelings about it.

- Stage 2: Anger
  You're resentful. (Why me?) Anger may be directed at the agency that imposed the change—boss, company, spouse, God—or displaced onto others or yourself.

- Stage 3: Bargaining
  You find yourself wishing for the old way, or scheming how to undo the change or get back what was lost. (*Example:* A child of a divorcing couple tries to influence his parents to get back together.)

- Stage 4: Depression
  This is the real work of grief: You are mourning the loss by being sad. At times you may feel overwhelmed or paralyzed by the loss.

- Stage 5: Acceptance
  You complete the work of the grief cycle. You've integrated the loss, and can reenter life and participate fully.

Grief counselors assure us that this model cannot be applied to every case. Also, that there is no right order to the grief stages. They often say, however, that "the only way out is through."

Code the Changes

This is the payoff step. Turn back to your list of changes, and mark each item on your change list that included a loss with a number from 1 to 5, according to the stage of grief you feel you are in right now with respect to that loss. For example, if you experience anger about the loss, mark the item with a 2; if you feel you've resolved your feelings about it, use a 5. (*Suggestion:* If you can't figure out what number to use, try a 1.)

Assess Results

Stand back from your work and see what value it's had for you.

- What is it telling you, that perhaps you knew vaguely before but now are clear about?
- How might applying the grief stages to changes help you understand yourself in the future?
- How might it explain what someone else you know is going through?
- What value might there be in communicating the results of this self-examination with someone?

As in every self-learning situation, take what you can get, and let the rest go by.

A Personal Story

"Despite everything you have achieved," writes David Whyte, "life refuses to grant you, and always will refuse to grant you, immunity from its difficulties." On the other hand, sometimes things that appear difficult are later seen to have been for the best. It's not knowing the ultimate outcome that makes it doubly hard to endure a difficulty. Something happened to me years ago that demonstrated a principle I've had occasion to call upon since: Sometimes it's right to say no to something without knowing why.

The best job offer I ever had (or so it appeared at the time) came when I was living in southern California and freelancing as a trainer for an organization that marketed seminars for teachers.

The proffered position would have assured me a top salary, much prestige, a large staff, and virtually unlimited power to create and implement a new curriculum design that would make a difference in the education of one of the largest city school systems on the East Coast. At the time I had no steady, reliable income. My family would have made the move okay. Nothing seemed to be in the way, yet I found myself delaying and fidgeting and avoiding the decision. Why was I hesitating?

Feeling terrible for causing those who had extended this generous offer to wait an unconscionably long time, I made a day-long business trip to Los Angeles. Driving home to San Diego later in the day, I found myself stalled in a huge traffic jam. As I sat there, looking over at those curiously bare hills along the Pacific shore, for the first time I seriously considered telling them no. Instantly my whole being was flooded with relief. I felt light as a feather. Arriving home, I told my wife to forget the move. (Perfect job . . . or no job at all? No comparison!)

As I continued to struggle along on my sporadic income as a freelancer I wondered sometimes if I'd made the right decision. Each time I was assailed with doubt I would recall that feeling of elation that swept over me when I considered turning the job down.

Months later I heard that the city school system in which I would have been working had I accepted was involved in painful labor disputes and a virtual uprising by parents against the very forces that would have hired me. Eventually the program lost its funding and had to dismiss all its staff. I had dodged a bullet. The greatest benefit of that experience, though, was that it confirmed me as a freelancer, my own boss, which I have been able to make into a satisfying career.

It is difficult to say no when the prospects seem favorable, yet often when the rational mind, and everybody around us, are pushing us to take a certain step, we need to reach inside and listen to our own quiet counsel. Then we need the courage to act with faith—the evidence of things not seen.

Mind Like Water Exercises

■ *Free Fall*

This is the mental equivalent of learning downhill skiing. Facing down a steep mountain, the tendency is to hang back, but skiing works counterintuitively: only when you put your weight over the ski tips and "fall" can you experience control with the edges. There is a drop zone below you. Let go and fly.

■ *Become Positively Addicted*

William Glasser's book *Positive Addiction* is a classic, and one that needs revisiting in turbulent times. The author cites examples of people who became hooked on something that built strength and well-being. If they neglected the activity they became unhappy, but as soon as they returned to it they glowed with well-being. Glasser's group included many runners and meditators; but any activity will do, as long as it fulfills the following conditions:

- It is perceived as adding value to you.
- You can do it alone.
- You can do it for at least twenty minutes a day.
- You can do it without any self-criticism.

The benefits of becoming "positively addicted" are curiously in sync with the needs of busy, harried people today. When you build strength through a routine task, you create inner reserves of calm strength and fortitude. You induce high self-esteem and at the same time achieve balance between alone time and being with others. Beyond those conditions, there's the twenty-one-day rule. If you can do your activity alone, for twenty minutes, without judgment, every day for twenty-one days straight, chances are you'll become positively addicted to it. You may quit, but you'll go back because you'll miss the feelings the activity provided.

■ Fear Only Fear

Times of great change are often scary for people. While some wake up and calmly greet each new morning with a smile and the words "Another day, O Lord," others open their eyes and cry "O Lord! Another day!" While it's true we can't control or change or predict the events that lie ahead on our path, we can impact the most critical factor, the one that determines how the whole day will be experienced. We can change our minds.

Fortify your mind against fear. The first thoughts that enter your mind upon awakening each morning are crucial. Avoid troubling thoughts by immediately placing your mind on a happy memory or person. Keep a book of positive sayings by the bed and read one first thing. Or practice an affirmation:

- *My mind is awake to all the goodness around me.*
- *I am submerged in peace and tranquillity.*
- *This day beckons me forward down a cool hallway of calmness.*

■ Do Endurance Training

There are things we must go through, times when there is no substitute for just hanging on. The loss of a loved one, a life-threatening disease, financial disaster—these are times when a person's mettle is tested, the character is hammered out. You cannot learn *about* endurance, you must endure to know that experience.

There are many ways you can develop inner strength by *practicing* endurance. Do something you think you cannot do. After succeeding in that, choose something harder. Once every two weeks, go on a day-long fast on orange juice and ground nuts. Go without sleep. Exceed your routine physical workout. Curb your spending. Put yourself in a place to *do without* and study your own consciousness.

■ Immunize Yourself against Adversity

If you are studiously avoiding all unpleasantness in your life, you are placing your happiness in jeopardy by the constant dread that some unavoidable setback is just around the corner. Give up living that way forever. Set a goal: serene fortitude in the face of disappointment. Use the strategy by which we immunize ourselves against certain diseases: stimulating the body's reserves to overactivity by taking toxins into the body in graduated doses. Immunize yourself against trouble by meeting and facing each unavoidable disappointment as it occurs. Walt Whitman:

> O joy of suffering!
> To struggle against great odds! To meet enemies undaunted!
> To be entirely alone with them! to find how much one can stand!
> To look strife, torture, prison, popular odium, death, face to face!
> To mount the scaffold! To advance to the muzzles of guns with perfect nonchalance!
> To be indeed a God!

■ Trust Life

These days there are many alarms, many voices telling us we can't trust, we shouldn't trust. Such fear frustrates our intelligence. Good performance is based on feeling good. The proper way is to take whatever precautions are necessary, then put fears to rest and enjoy yourself.

No one would invite adversity into his or her life, but wise men and wise women throughout the ages have agreed that hard times forge character by teaching us to endure. Many metaphors point to this—steel tempered in flame, the Great Barrier Reef coral, a tree bending in a gale. Using the aquanamous mind, we can know that nothing happens by accident, that every trial bears a gift, and that often that gift is the opportunity to build strength of heart and mind by bearing strain.

STEP 24

Live Your Dream

A goal is a dream with a deadline.

—MARGIE BLANCHARD

Often when people talk about the realest, sharpest moments in their lives, they say, "It was as if I was in a dream." Perhaps without realizing it, they are touching on a profound truth. Maybe the realest moments tune us into timeless time, spaceless space where our Real Selves dwell. Maybe all the rest of that time we call waking life or "reality" is actually processed *un*reality. Maybe when as youngsters we sang the familiar round "Row, row, row your boat gently down the stream; Merrily, merrily, merrily, merrily, life is but a dream," we were expressing a profound truth.

As a child I always believed that life was a dream. Each experience seemed tinged with the same surreal quality I experienced when I was nightdreaming. As succeeding decades of my life brought increased responsibilities, that dreamlike sensation receded. Now, at a more advanced age, I find it is back, stronger than ever. Each day I welcome my childlike belief that "life is but a dream" and receive its benefits.

A dream view of the world affords relief and an important detachment from the highs and lows of experience, allowing a part of one's consciousness to be removed during painful conditions, so as to merely observe. Dreamers are able to keep their "cool" when others lose theirs, to be not too lifted up during elation nor too swept away by loss. When I purposely practice seeing life as a dream, certain events become invested with magic. A hidden presence breathes from behind all things, peering at me in the blossoms of flowers, or speaking to me out of a child's laughter.

You Are in Your Dream, I Am in Mine

There is another, less mystical, way of conceptualizing a dreamlike world that is not metaphysical but psychological. That is, the very way each individual looks at the world can be seen as his or her own private dream. For each living person, everything in the universe that is happening right now, is happening in his or her thought. There are various ways to express this: You create your own reality. Perception is all there is. What you see is what you get. Reality is a private affair. Consciousness is the only game in town.

People talk confidently of objective reality, but the only way we perceive reality is through our experience, which is subjective. Thus each of us is moving in the dream of his or her own subjective reality. Also, like the nocturnal dreamer, we can be said to be making it all up—for us things are only the way we see them, colored by our individual beliefs and expectations.

Connecting with the Myth of Life

Besides the mystical and the psychological definitions of world as dream, a third and most intriguing concept adds depth to the matter. It is the *mythical* explanation of human experience. Carl Jung spent a good part of his life studying dreams—his own, those of his patients, and those in other cultures. He wrote, "One does not dream; one is dreamed. We undergo the dream; we are the objects." Assimilating his studies of thousands of dreams, Jung posited the notion of the *collective unconscious,* a shared mythology that is always present and is acted out beneath conscious awareness through members of a culture.

It's not difficult to substitute the word "dream" for "myth" in this context. Jungian analyst Robert Johnson explains: "The myth is the thing you're in and don't know it's a myth. Myth is what captures your imagination and moves your language and your body into doing things in certain ways. So we're always in myth." Science and technology can be said to be our present myth. As great masses of people move about using electronic means of instant communication, they focus on the tools—computers, Internet, satellites, cell phones, and pagers. All the while they may be, dreamlike, fulfilling the racial mission of linking the planet as never before.

I like this explanation of life as a story in which we are all acting parts, and we don't know that we are the story characters. Like Jung and Campbell, I'm intrigued by what is behind and beneath, the play of unseen forces.

Benefits of "Dream Consciousness"

Yogananda declared that the greatest thing you can do to cultivate wisdom is to practice the consciousness of the world as a dream. The more one practices this perception, the stronger becomes the realization that it is not an unrealistic or a pathological escape, but a way of contacting reality. Far from denying responsibility, it affords a way to take in one's experience with acceptance and a healthy detachment. If life is a dream, perhaps we "wake up" each night when we sleep. Sleep is a mystery even to neuroscientists.

There are groups and cultures who have believed for centuries that sleep is not primarily for rest, but our way of regularly getting back to the truth of our souls. Otherwise, they say, we could not deal with the misery and tragedy of waking existence.

Re-mind Yourself

Make an experiment. Choose a routine week and determine to live it in the consciousness that it is a dream. Whenever you think of it, tell yourself, *It is only a dream.* The goal of the experiment should be to discover what, if any, difference it makes to regard your own waking experience as a dream. Keep a journal during this time and make notes like any scientist. What was different today? What was the same? Did dreaming the world help or benefit me? How?

Use Dream Consciousness to Find Peace

A couple with a new baby noticed that their three-year-old daughter spent much time alone with the newborn, talking to her in whispers. Concerned, the parents decided to listen in over the nursery intercom. They heard the little girl saying, "Tell me again what it's like where we come from. I'm already starting to forget."

This world can appear so real and so frightening, for it is to reason and logical perception that we wake each day, to the world's arrows and indignities. But sages speak of a "peace that passes understanding," that lies outside of reason, beyond all that our senses insist is true. "The things of earth grow strangely dim" when one sits quietly and goes deeply within to rest in it. That peace, that ever-new joy, is not merely a feeling or a hope or a belief—it is a realization. (Oh, this was here all the time! This truth lay just behind all the hurts and buffetings of the world, and I did not know it. That is, I knew it as a child, for I came from it—but I forgot it.) It takes a wake-up like this for us to seek again that reality of our selves.

Conquer Fear

Whenever you are worried or fearful, like a small child having a nightmare, use the dream idea to dispel the threat. (After all, if it's only a dream, you can't really be hurt.) Tell yourself that you are playing a part in the scenario of a cosmic dreamer. Try to feel what that part is and should be in the moment, and concentrate on getting out of the way and being "played through."

"Well," you say, "whether it's a dream or not, I must go to work, buy food, pay bills, and keep out of the way of passing cars." That's true. This dream is a very real-seeming one—true to smell, taste, sound, sight, and touch. Especially when tragedy strikes, there can seem no respite from its hard reality. That's when it's time to do like the little girl in the story: try to go within and remember. We all came from someplace, and we're all going back.

Take Little Naps

Why should nighttime be the only time we snooze? Often after rising early and working many hours, I grab a short afternoon nap. As I awaken from a deep, refreshing sleep, I sometimes feel I've been somewhere more real than the environment in which I wake, and brought back an extraordinary level of refreshment and renewal.

Dreams as Aspirations

We often use "dream" to denote high aspiration. I am intrigued by the power of dreams to draw us to greater heights of being and doing. Virtually everybody, given the chance to find it, has a dream of shining possibility. The ability to dream—to imagine, to visualize, to see in our mind's eye where we want to come out—is what keeps us going through difficulties. Visualizing our goal clearly, we can avoid being sidetracked or being drawn away to a lesser goal. Often the key person in a team or an organization is the one who is the "dreamkeeper," the one whose vision of the preferred outcome is clear, and who inspired others with this clarity.

Over the years I've often found myself able to use the notion of the dream to help people communicate and clarify their ideals. When I am listening to someone who is complaining of a difficulty or sharing something that is frustrating, I ask the person, "So, what's your dream?" (In other words: If all obstacles were out of the way; what would you aspire to achieve?) At this point a predictable pattern plays out. The person pauses, looks briefly at me, then looks up and to the side. A slight smile, a sigh, or a sitting back, and the dream emerges. As the heart's desire is put into words, the person's appearance is altered; by getting in touch with high aspiration the soul comes to the fore.

I have a dream. Someday I want to write something that will uplift the whole human race and further it toward the next step of evolution in consciousness. In my dream this work releases the best that is in people, causing their light to shine more brightly in the world. I visualize this work as divinely inspired—that is, it will not be original in the usual sense of that term. It will not come from me at all, but rather will simply utilize my skills and energies as instruments. It would have to be that way because this work will open the universal wisdom and light that is in all of us.

That's my dream. But there's a problem. I've noticed that often my writing tends to come out preachy or condescending. That's when it's coming from the ego, the false little self in me wanting to take credit and claim power and omniscience. (It's helpful to think of the ego as an alias, a sort of psychic Halloween costume, if you will, from behind which we can step out, so as to view things clearly and dispassionately.) This imposter can defeat my purpose. To achieve my dream I will have to watch and pray, asking that whenever the ego takes over, it be revealed to me. Only when I wake up to it can I step aside from it. In this way I can move toward achieving my dream in practical terms.

Mind Like Water Exercises

■ *Share Your Dream*

When you frame your dream in actual language, it takes on more energy and reality. Clothing it in words causes you to have to visualize it. As you see the dream emerge, you add details to it. Describing it in detail gives you the feeling of having the dream come true already. This is why the process of telling someone your dream moves you forward, brings you closer to actualizing your dream. Tell someone your dream, and ask them to tell you theirs.

An added bonus of sharing your dream is that it builds your confidence. When your listener does not question or make light of the dream, but rather understands and identifies with it, you tell yourself, "It must not be that crazy." Also, it's likely that by hearing what you deeply want, your listener will have ideas and suggestions that will support your doing what you dream of doing, having what you dream of having, being what you dream of being.

Sometimes when I am coaching a group or conducting a workshop I ask people to pair up and take turns asking each other, "What's your dream?" I say, "When your partner is sharing his or her dream, give that person your undivided attention. Don't interrupt or ask questions. When the dream has been shared, take a few moments and say back what you heard, to show you got it." For homework, I've assigned each participant to tell someone else their dream who does not know it. I recall one man who came back the following day and shared that he'd told his wife his dream, and asked her what hers was. "We'd never done this," he said excitedly. "Now each of us is committed to supporting the other in achieving our dreams." The energy and enthusiasm with which he spoke told me that there had been real renewal in that relationship.

■ *Do the Dreamwork*

Unless you are an enlightened master you have an ego, a pseudo-self that wants to put itself forward, that takes things personally, takes offense, etc. The energy and activity of that little self can obliterate contact with the Dreamer within, the soul. It is the soul that dreams, and it is the soul that must bring the dream to pass. At every step along the way toward realizing your dream, you must be vigilant. Watch out for feelings of wanting to take credit. Be especially alert during times when you are stressed, frustrated, excited, elated, or depressed. Recognize these as symptoms of the little self, and ask for the grace to step aside from it. Affirm: *I serve this dream. This dream is doing me.*

To whatever extent we utilize the notion of the world as dream, it is certain that we all require some means of working within our minds to be able to shift perspective, even temporarily, from the tragic and the sorrowful that can defeat us. The aquanamous mind is your resource in dreaming and making dreams happen. The more you train yourself in the tools and the steps of the Mind Like Water growth process, the more in touch you will be with your deepest, highest, heartfelt ideals.

What's your dream? Tell somebody. And then remember that achieving that dream will require a change in your consciousness. Your dream requires you to serve it, to bow your ego to it. It will ask you to find out what in you stands in the way of achieving your goal, so you know what to rise above or step aside from. That's the real daily work of bringing your dream to actualization.

> Whatever you can do, or dream you can, begin it. Boldness has genius, power, and magic in it. Begin it now.
>
> —JOHANN VON GOETHE

AFTERWORD

The strongest thing in the entire universe—stronger than all the armies, stronger than all the massed might of the world—is an idea whose time has come.

—VICTOR HUGO

In his book *Tertium Organum,* the nineteenth-century Russian writer-philosopher P. D. Ouspensky compared ordinary consciousness to that of a blind man feeling about with a stick and making assumptions about the world from that limited experience. It has taken humankind more than a century to even begin to wake up to what he was saying. Using our technology, we have painted ourselves into a mental corner from which there is no escape. The information age, with its attendant speedup in change, has arrived to force us to transcend our primitive mental tools.

Familiar plaints of our driven world of work—*Too much on my plate! Too many balls in the air!*—suggest that our problem is the number of things we have to think about. Not so. As usual, it is our limited perception of things, not things themselves, that is off. The situation in which our species finds itself requires more than a new, modernized way of thinking that will equip us to deal with the overload of information and the paucity of time. Instead, we are headed toward a place that transcends thinking altogether.

237

Search for Transcendence

Western society's overemphasis on the externals of life—on analysis, logic, rationality, and hierarchy—has neglected the internal forces that can make even routine daily life vivid and ecstatic. Even though the psychic bind in which we currently find ourselves is painful, it is pointing us in the right direction. We are realizing our need for an ecstatic dimension to life.

Jung said that ecstasy is an archetypal quality, which is to say that humans are made for transcendence. Many of our common human miseries are actually traceable to this need. We are made to seek the spiritual, and if we don't get our ecstasy in a legitimate way, we will get it in illegitimate ways. "What people seek in addictive experience is normal," says Dr. Jeffrey Satinover. "The craving for certain kinds of elation, for a certain sense of specialness, for heroism, for cessation of pain. Underlying all of that is the seeking of a sense of meaningfulness."

Jung recognized that the key to the beginning of an addiction is the seeking of spirit. Alcoholics Anonymous, in fact, traces its origins to Jung's diagnosis of an allegedly incurable alcoholic known only as Roland H. Jungian specialist Dr. Robert Johnson declares that the metaphor of height applied to a mental state (as in the so-called mountaintop experience) is universal. "But when an individual seeks the experience of getting high," he adds, "the implication is that he or she chronically does not feel high."

The Big Left Turn

> Nothing is weaker than water,
> But when it attacks something hard,
> Or resistant, then nothing withstands it,
> And nothing will alter its way.
>
> —LAO TZU, *The Way of Life*

Throughout the time of generating the material for *Mind Like Water* and putting it into book form, I experienced the certainty that it was not "my" book—that this project has a life of its own. As the date for its publication arrived, I felt like a mother whose baby had been born and was now out in the world on its own, able to do whatever he or she was sent to do. I continue to feel that the book has "written me" instead of the other way around. I've merely been the instrument, and the job is to serve whatever's supposed to come through at the time.

I view this book project as one of the possible helping forces to the human race as it makes its Big Left Turn along about now in human history in the journey of evolving consciousness. Recently in a speech I mentioned the Big Left Turn. Afterward a gentleman said, "You really mean Right Turn, don't you?" That challenge invoking "rightness" reminded me that we are on our way, but we have a long way to go. The left side is controlled by the right brain, and the right side (not only right-handedness, but also in our our language "being right" and "writing") is under the control of the left brain. That's the part of us that wants to be right about everything, to have the ducks in a row, to use time-bound linear problem-solving, etc. We're growing the undeveloped "lefty" side of our minds, and these white-water times have come along to force us to use it.

Spiritually speaking, the evolution of consciousness is just a getting back to what we really are. Waking up and remembering. Coming out of our aliases and mistaken identities. Putting off being cosmically forgetful about our true identity. This is reinforced for me by the writings of masters such as Yogananda, who declared, "Noumenal truths cannot be understood by the sensory mind. Phenomena can be interpreted by the intellect from sensory experience, but not the substance, or noumena, underlying it.... If one can gain access to his inherent discriminative intelligence, he can arrive at the inner comprehension of truth that is attainable only by the spiritual development of the soul's intuitive powers of perception."

What sort of preparation can people possibly make in order to move toward such a state? It is to respond to this important question that this present book is offered. A great Native American chief was speaking to his tribe members as they faced the takeover of their way of life by the white man. He told them that the change that was coming was like a great river that they must enter with faith and confidence, trusting that the water knew where it was going. He counseled them to be fearless and welcoming of the change: "Let go," he said. "Push off into the middle. Keep your head up."

The Big Left Turn is like an implacable river that will sweep us along with its force. We could hang back, but that would only cause us more pain and delay our making the changes that are necessary. In our becoming what we are meant to be, we too in these chaotic times must let go, push off, and keep our heads up.

INDEX